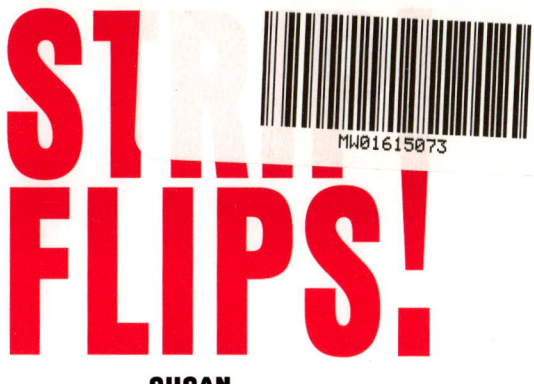

STREET FLIPS!

SUSAN

by Leslie Lyons

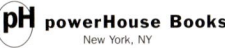

pH **powerHouse Books**
New York, NY

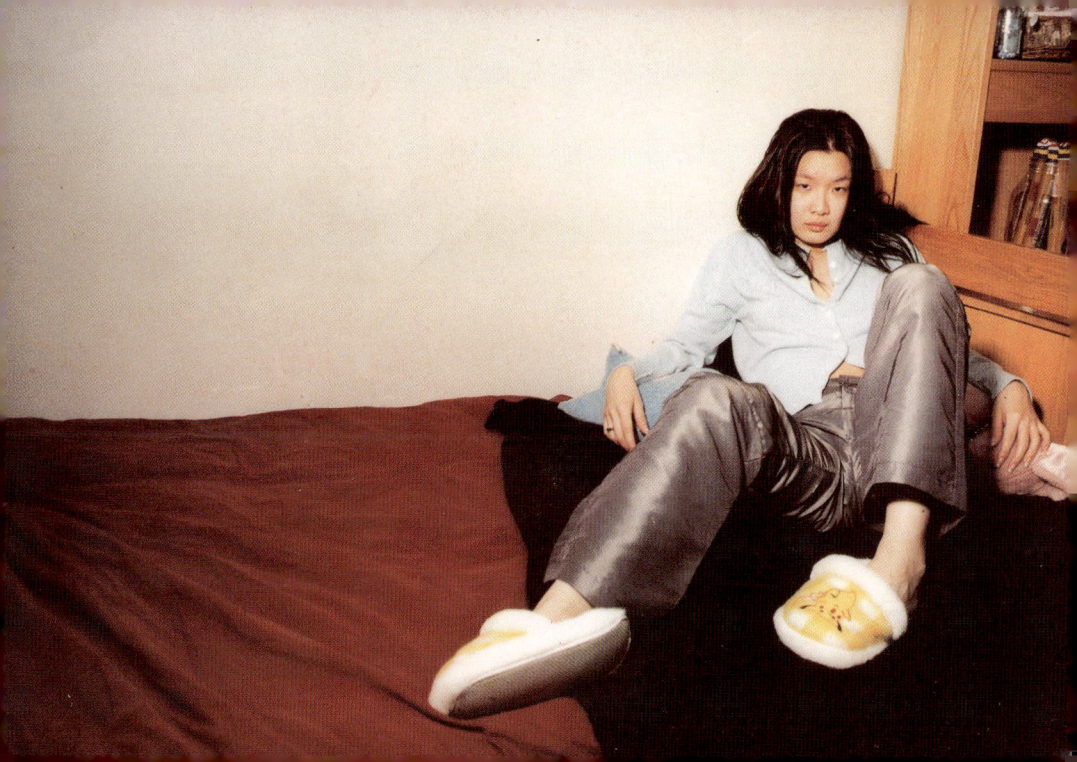

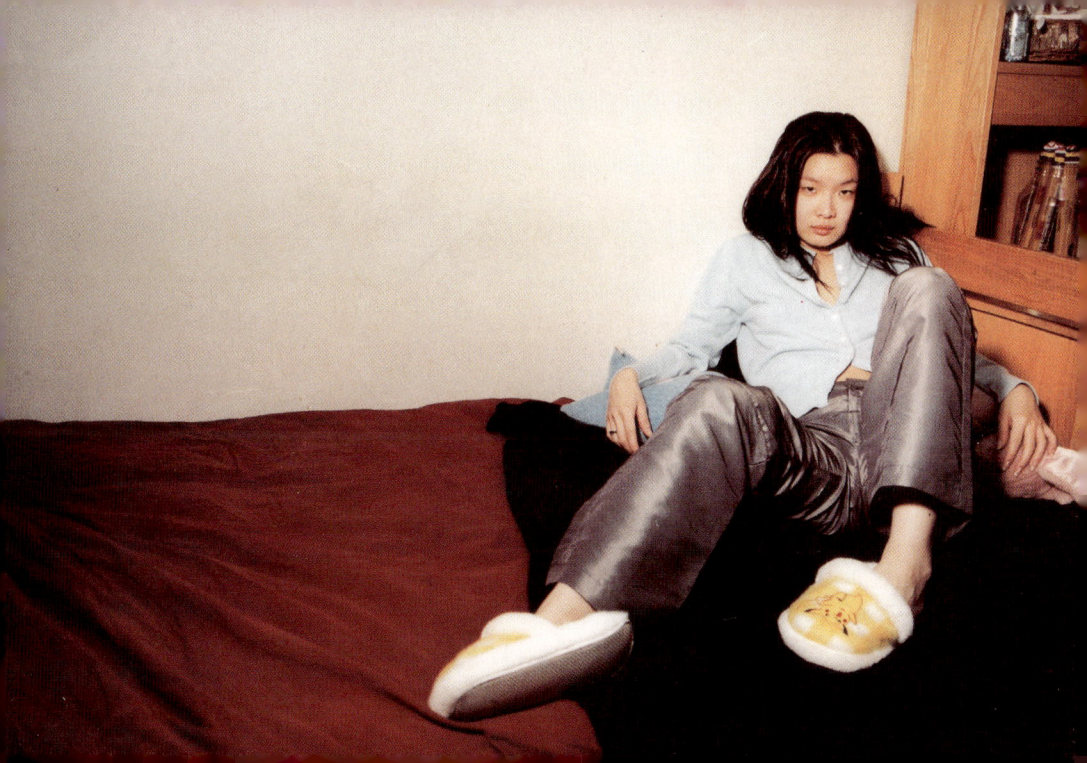

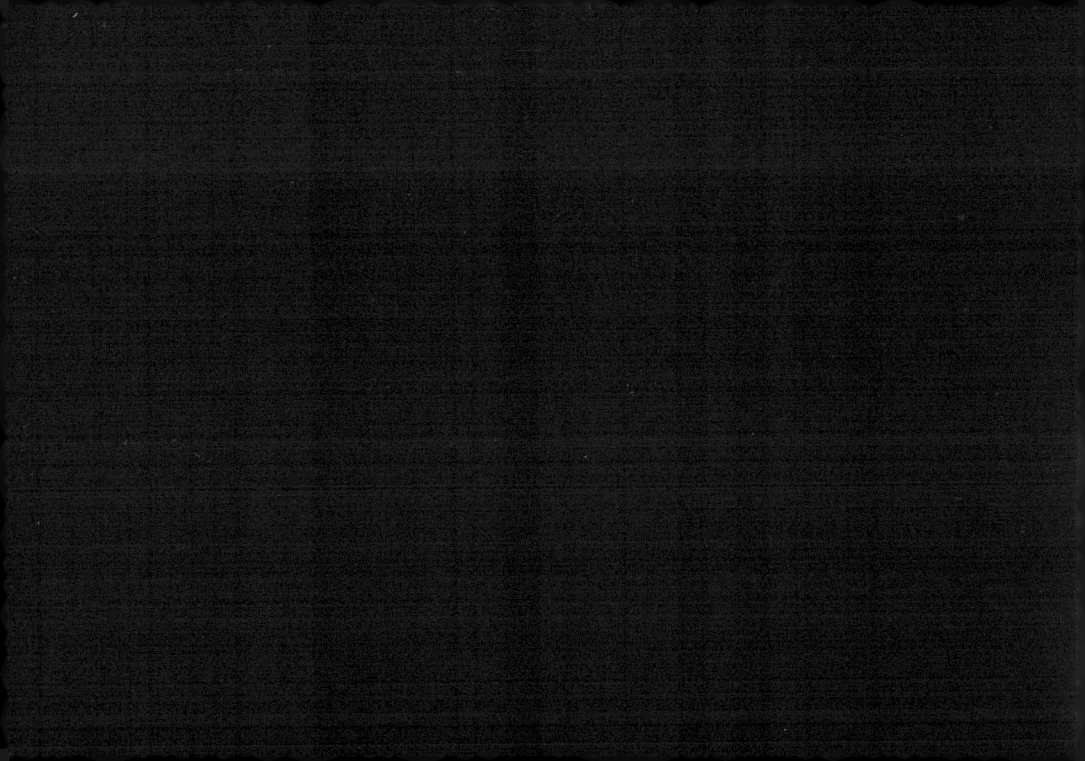

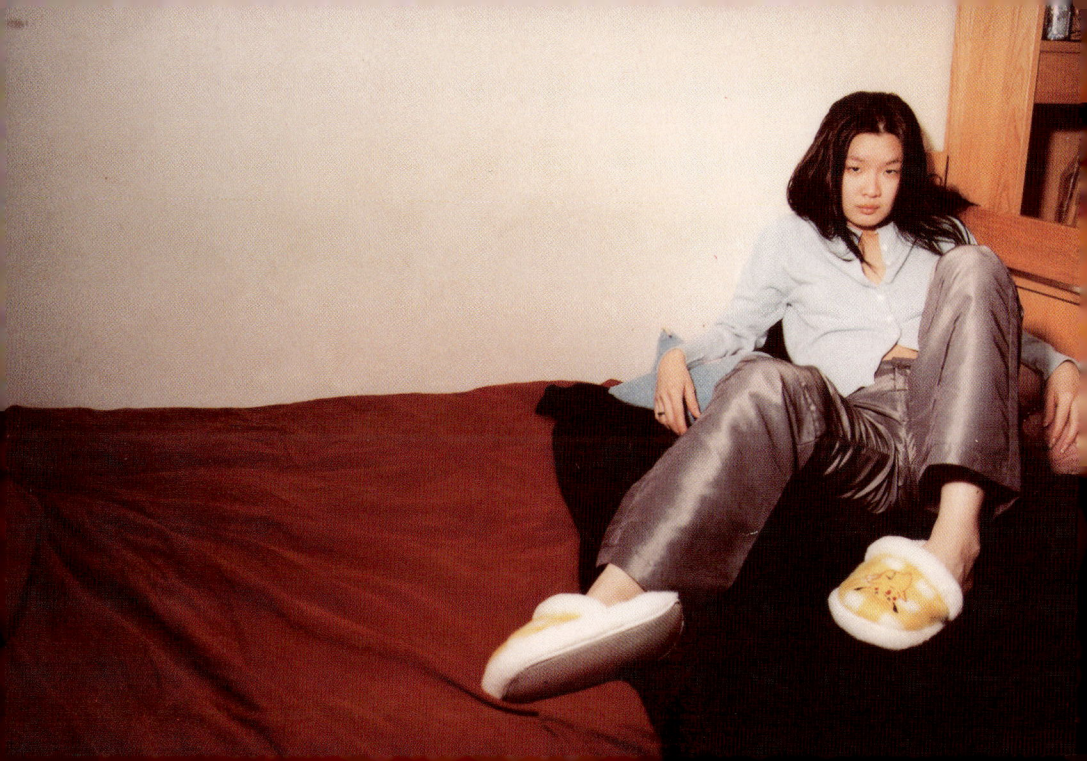

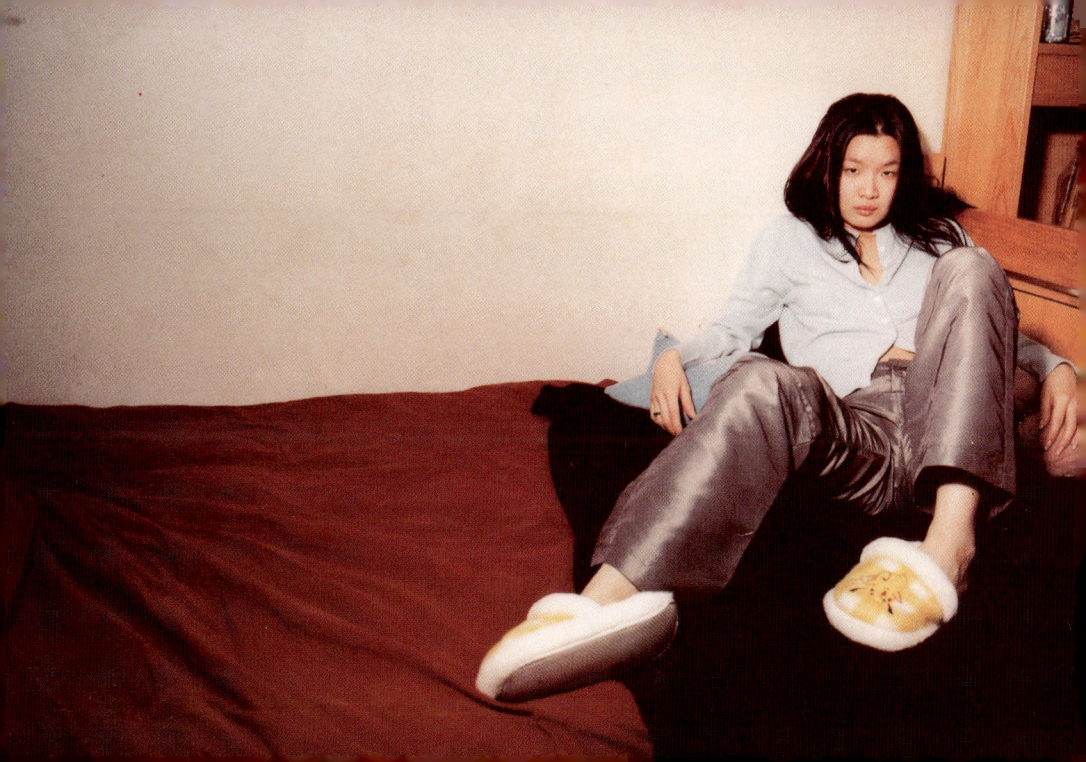

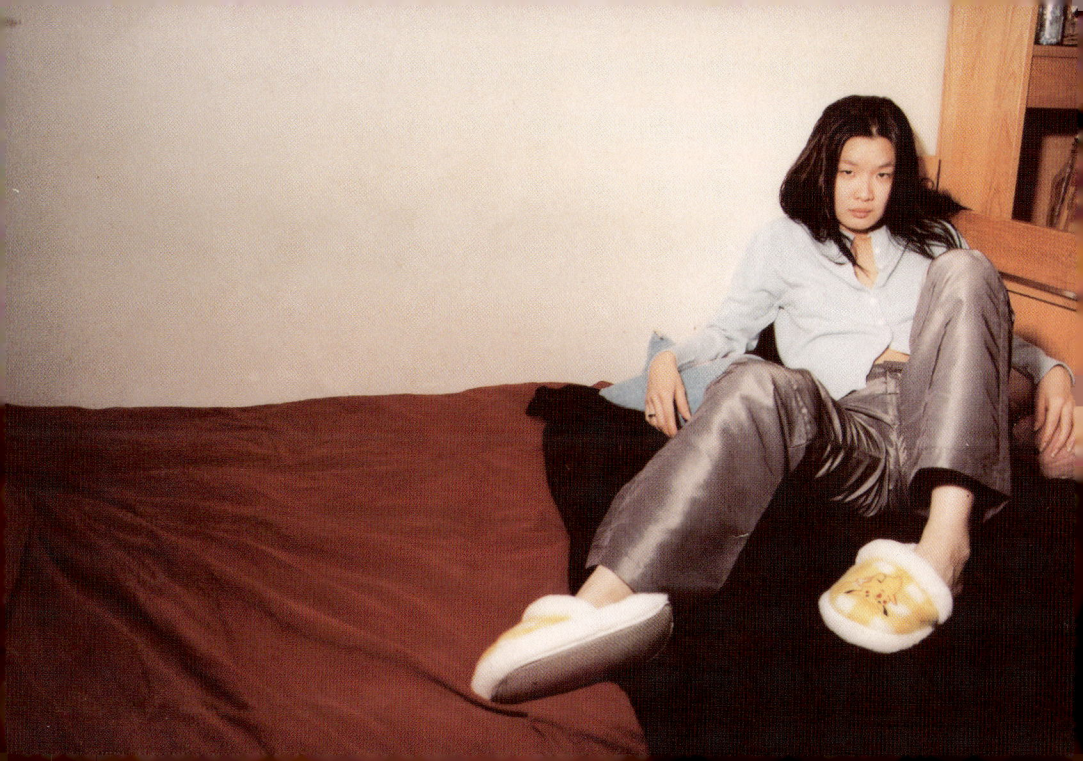

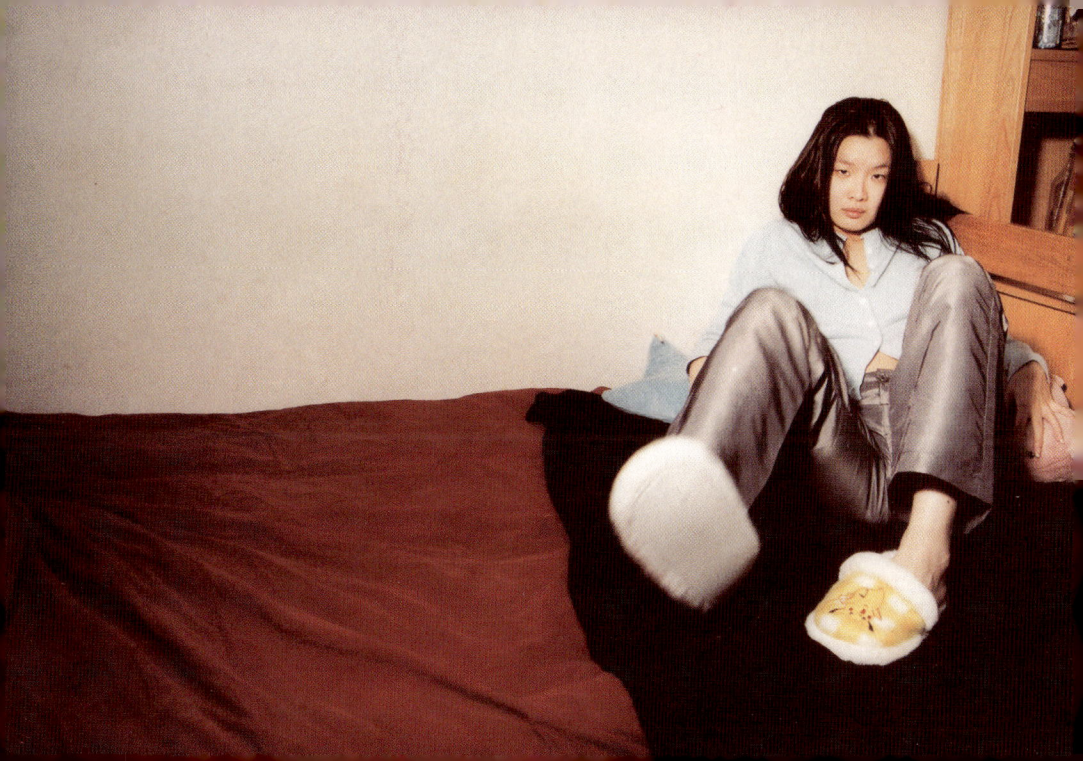

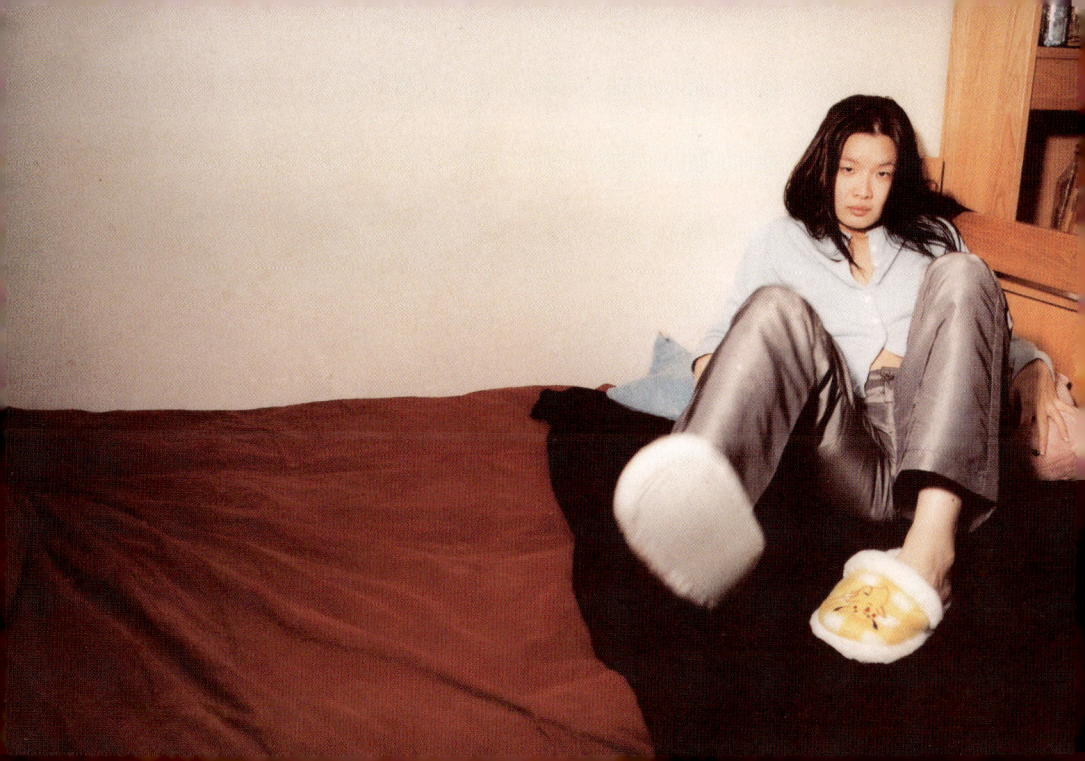

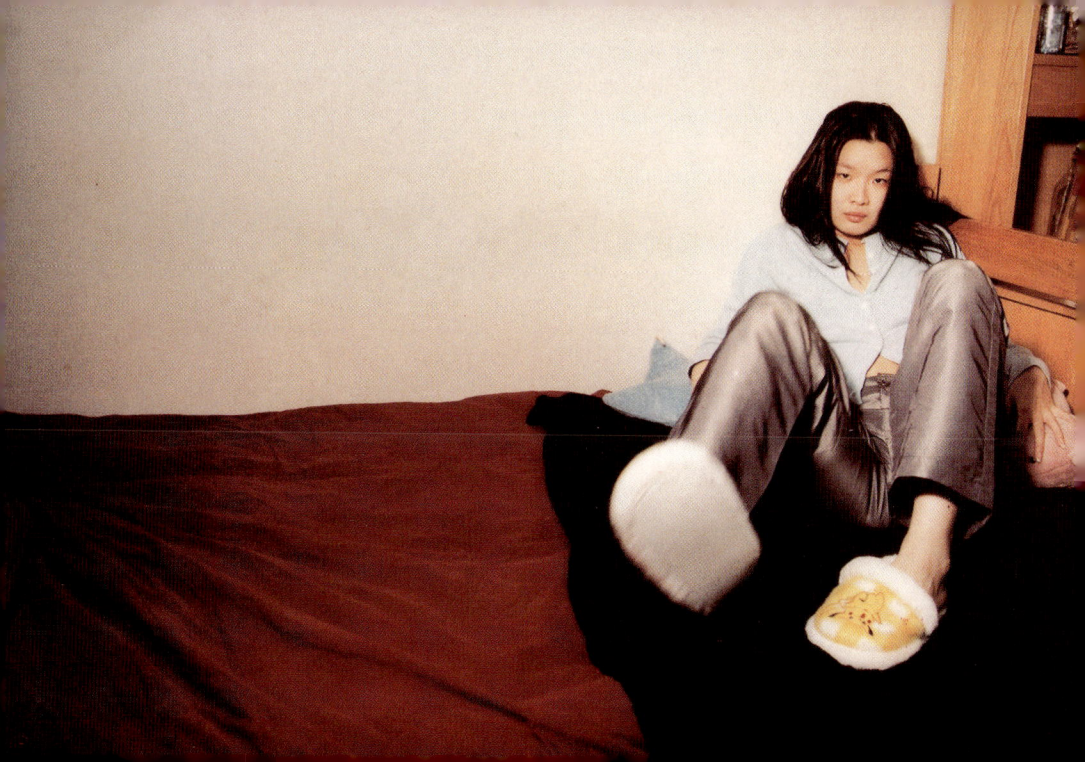

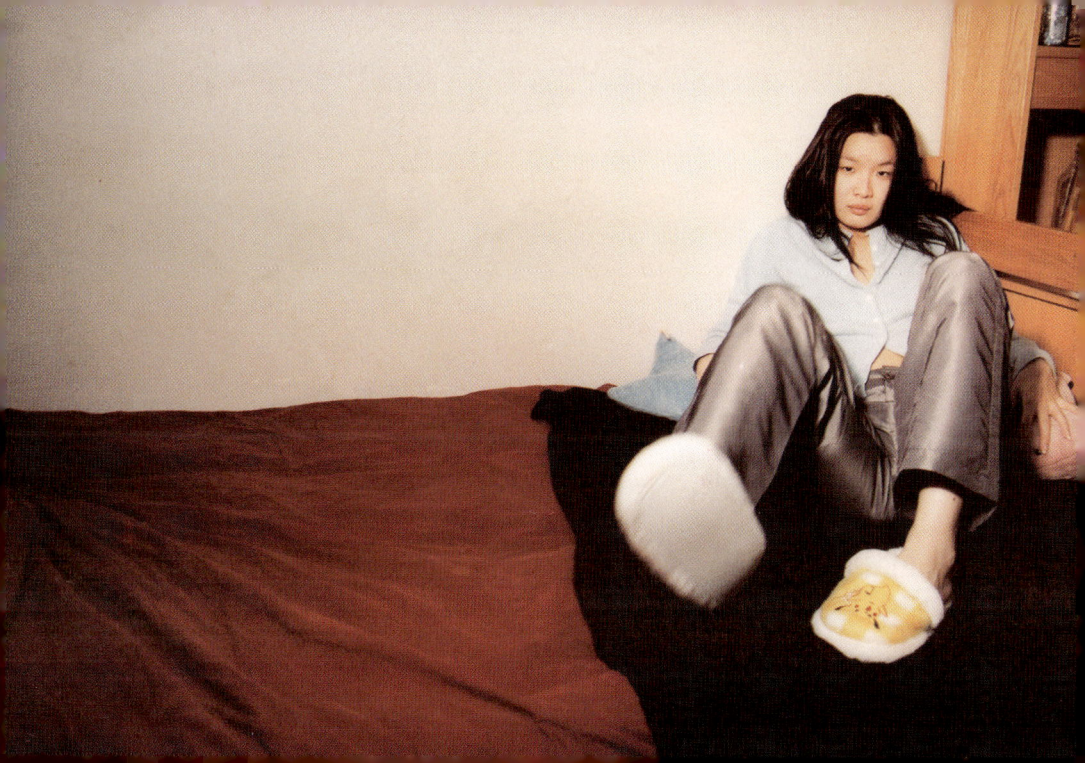

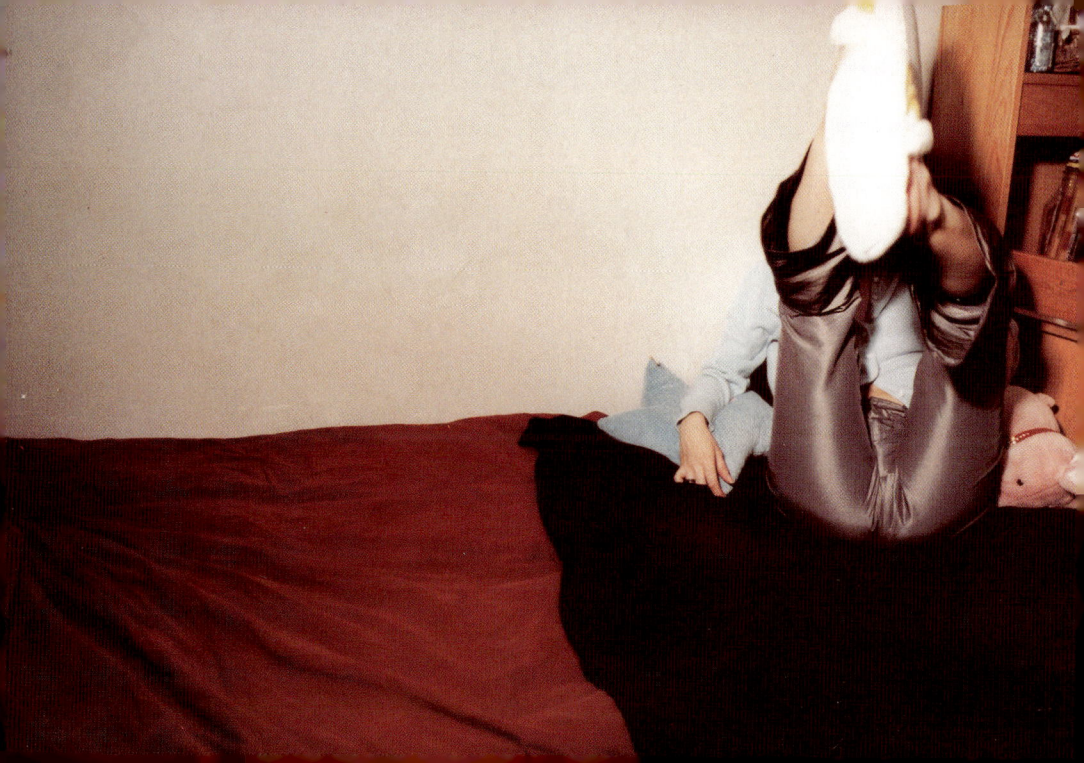

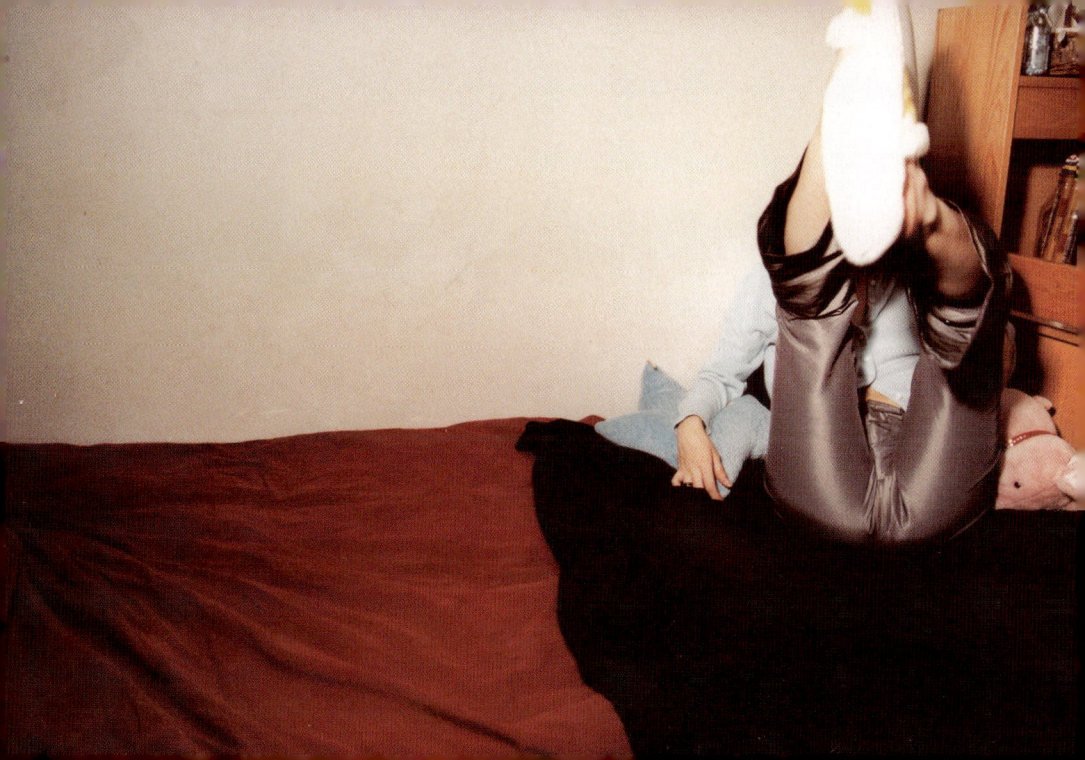

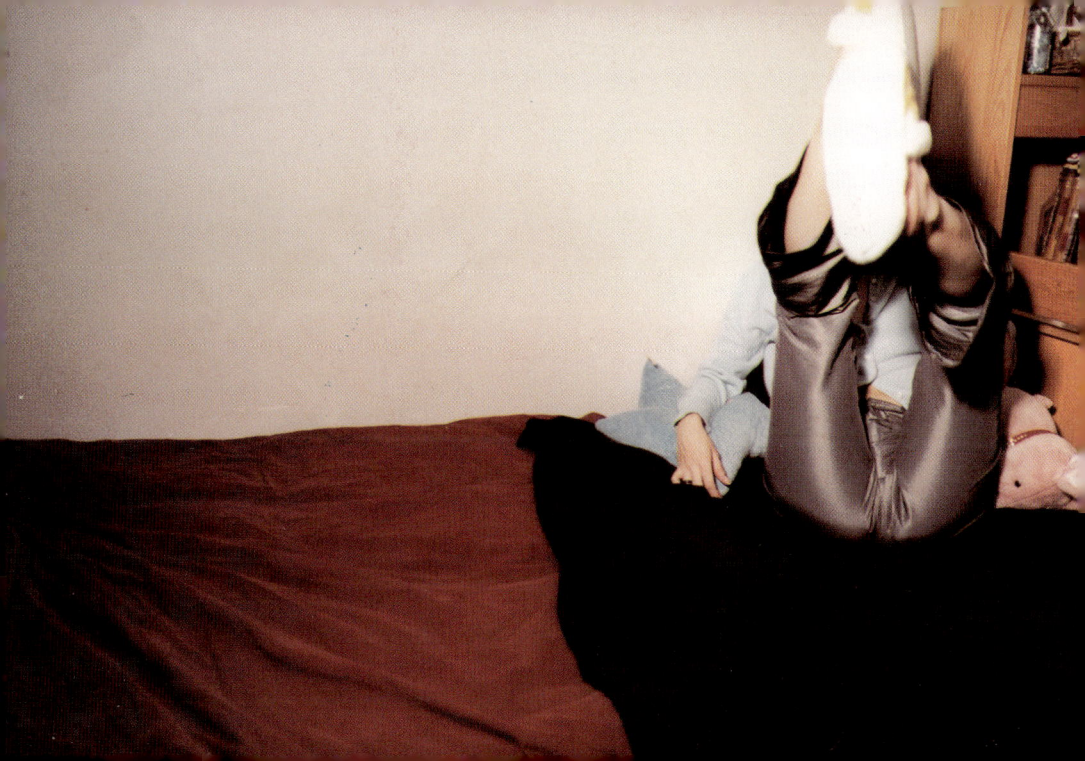

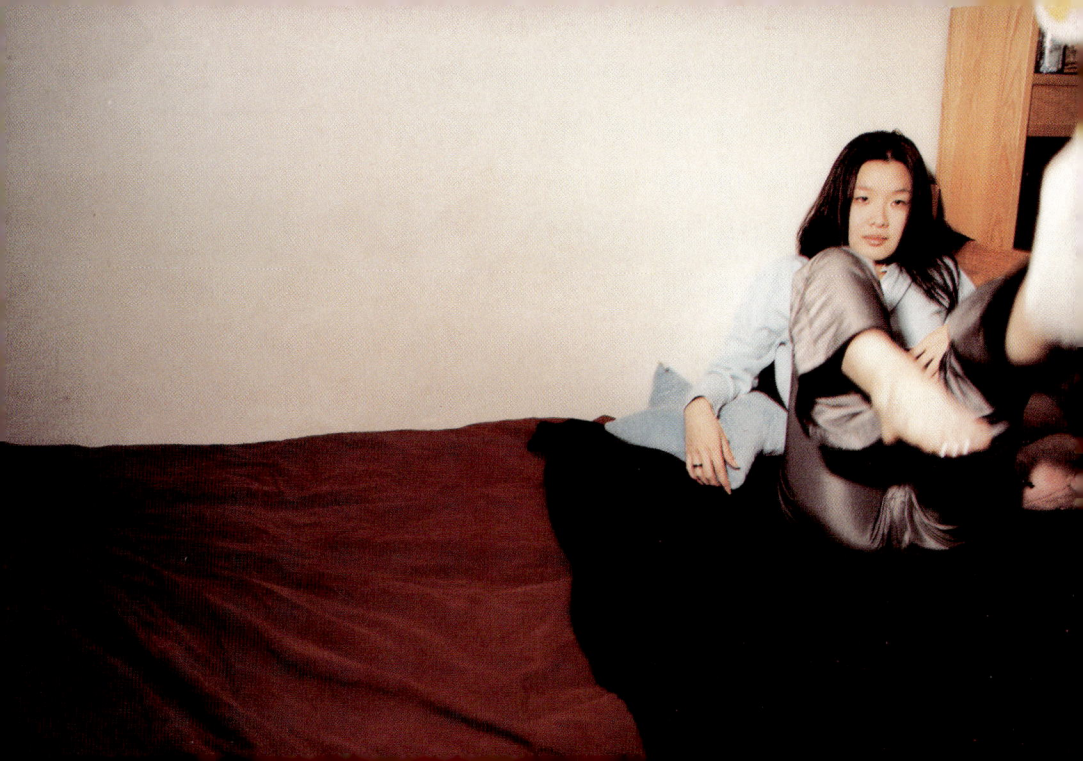

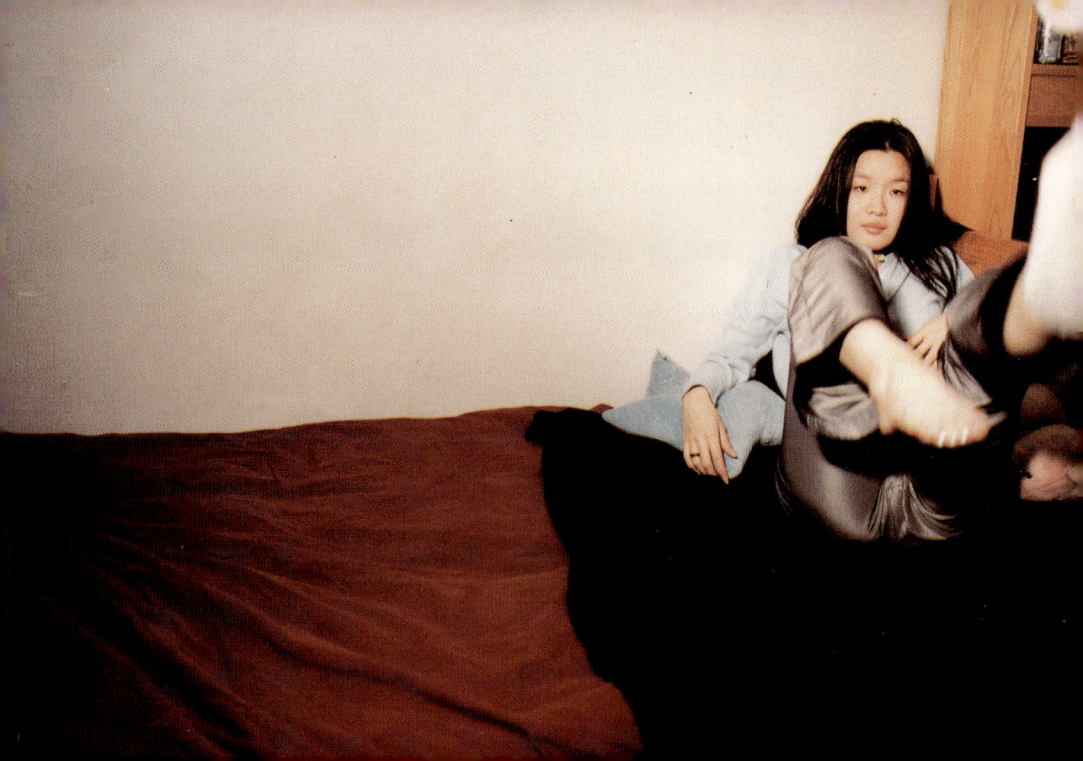

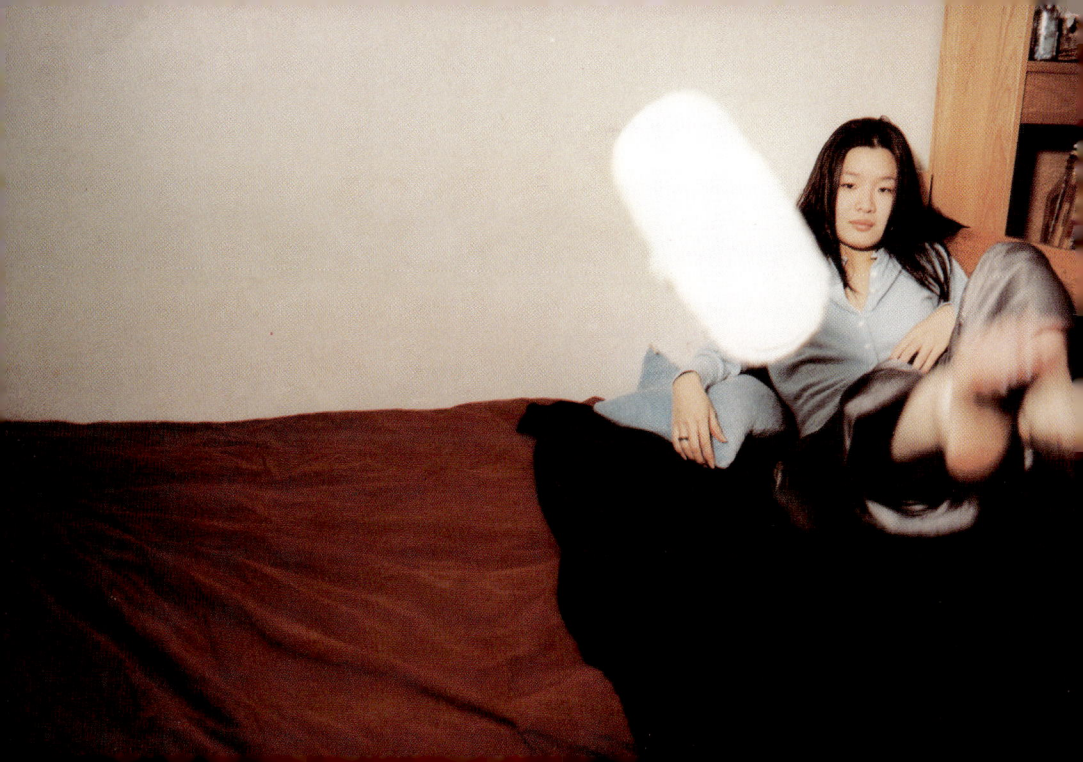

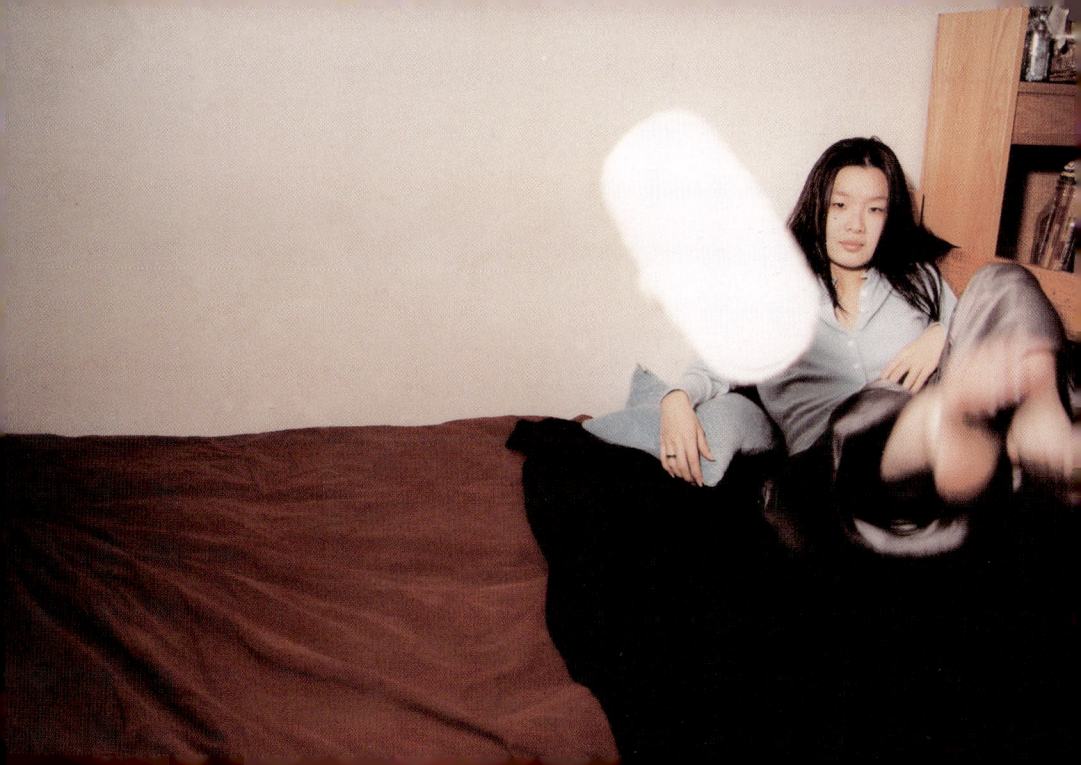

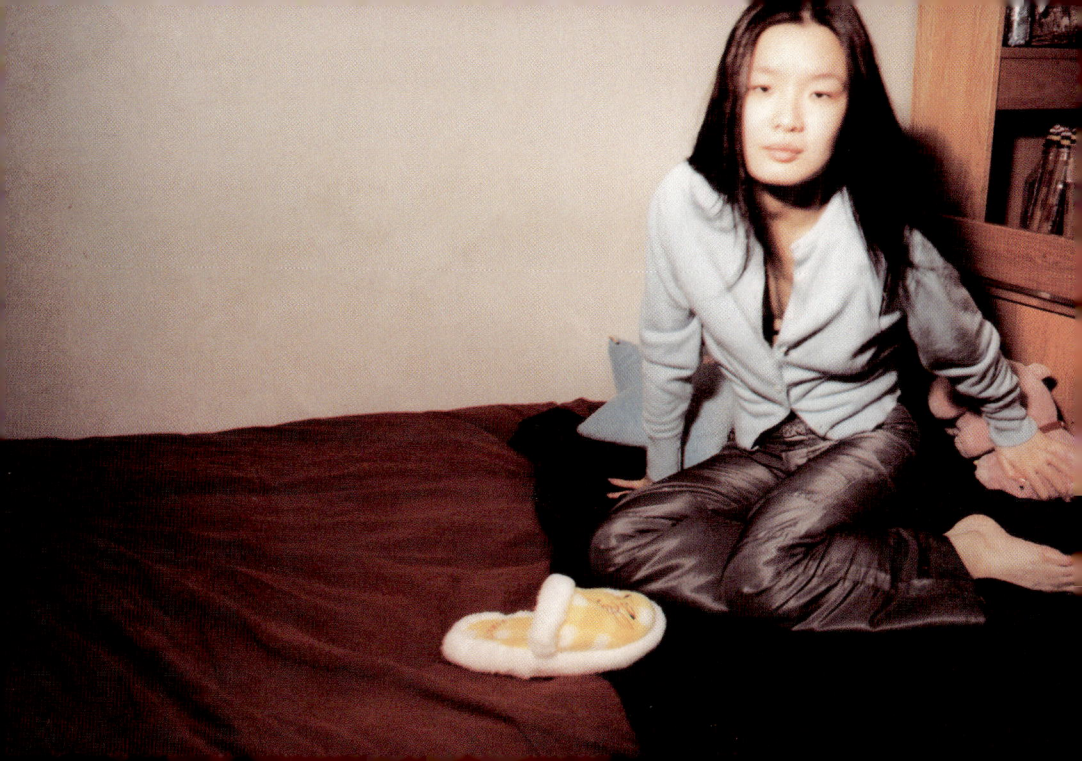

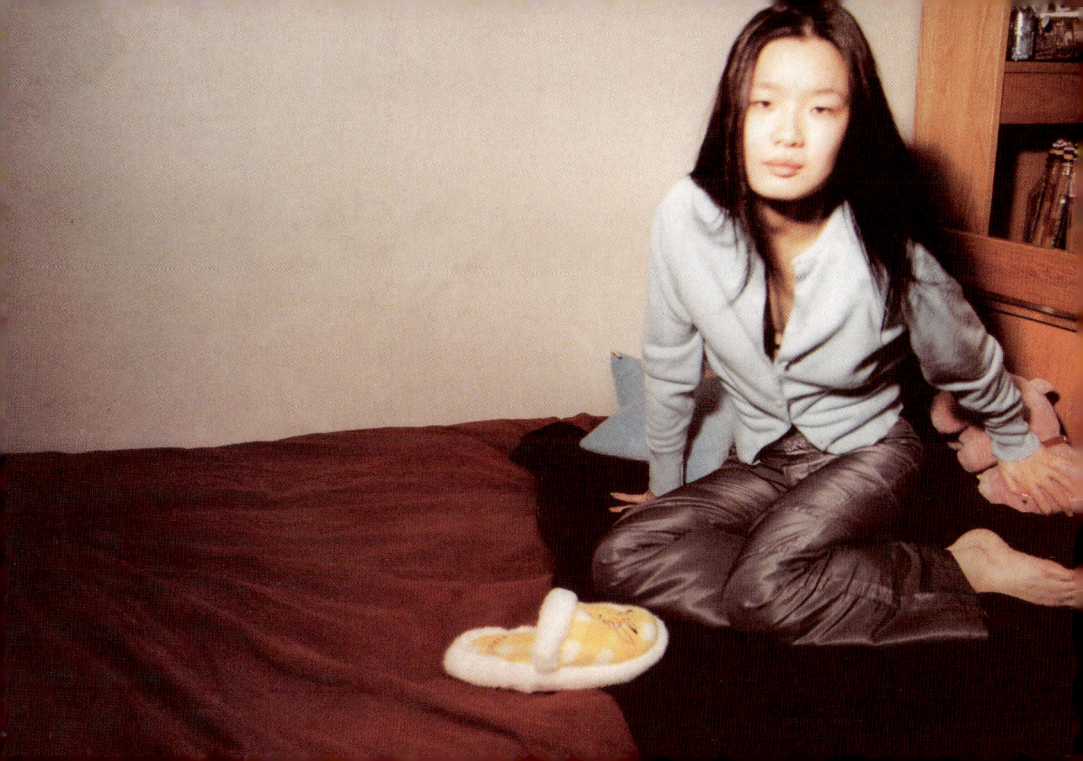

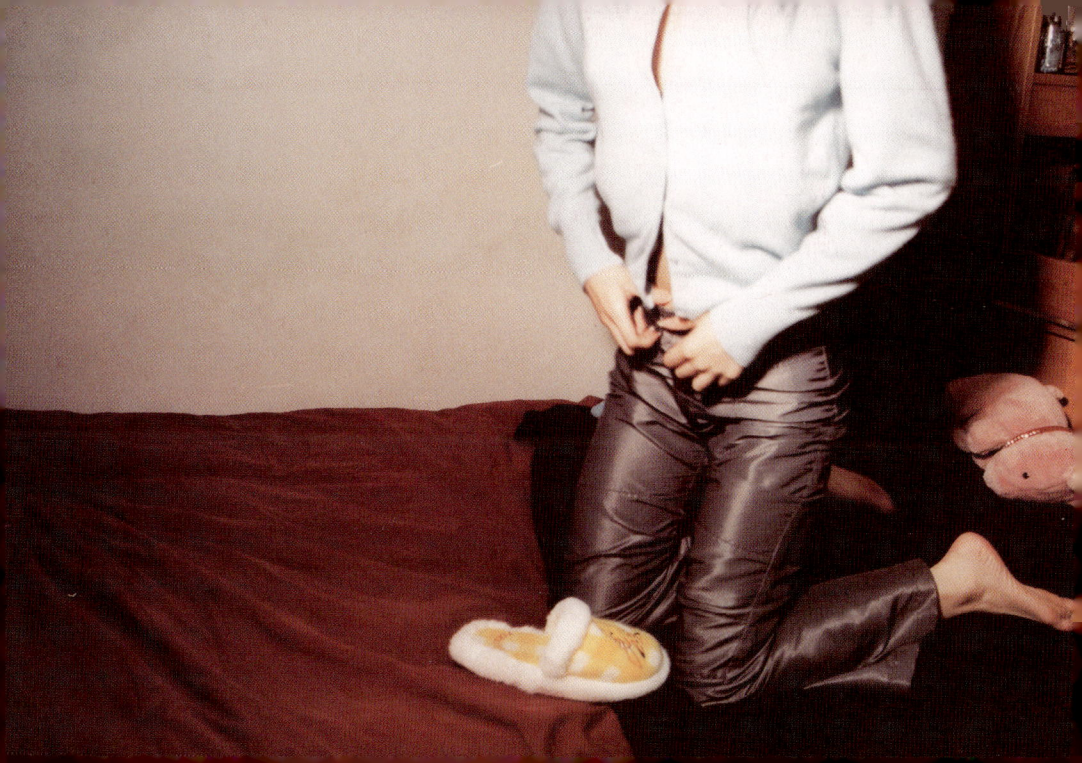

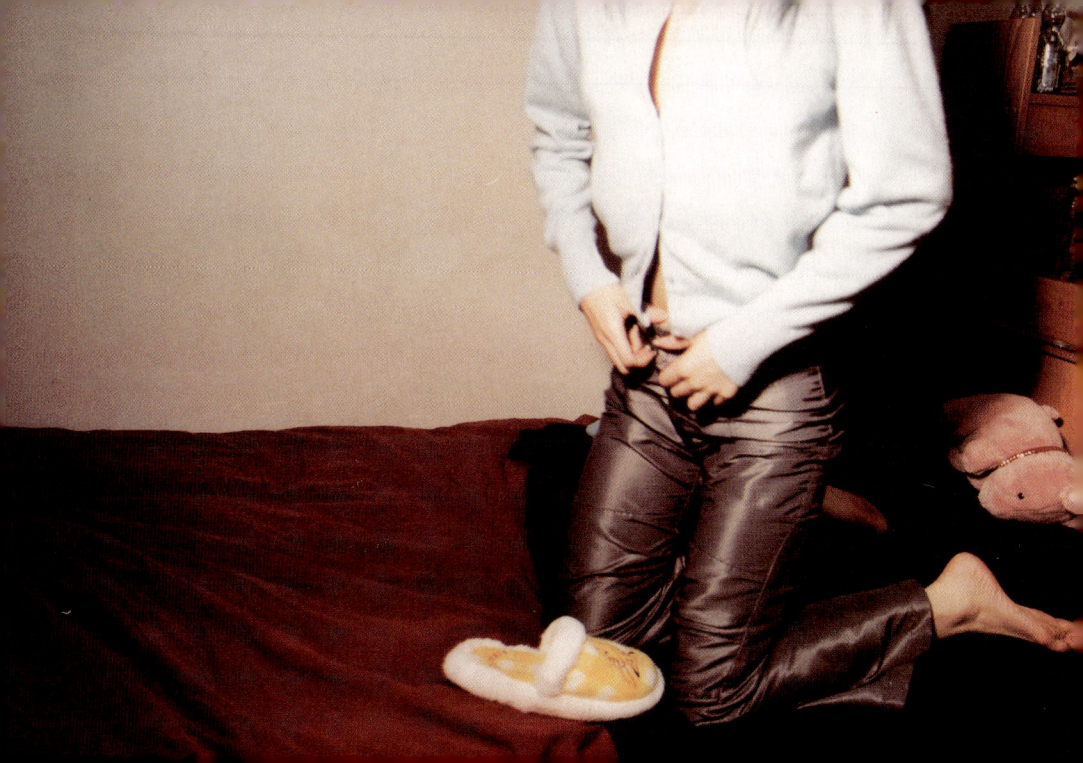

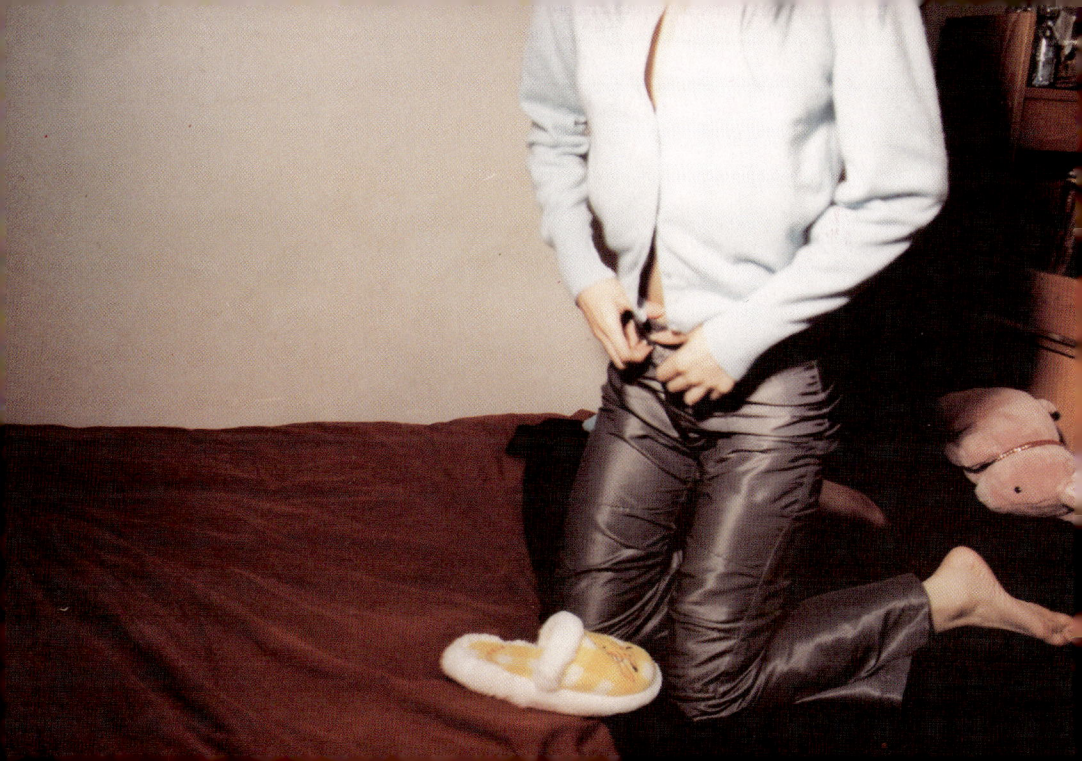

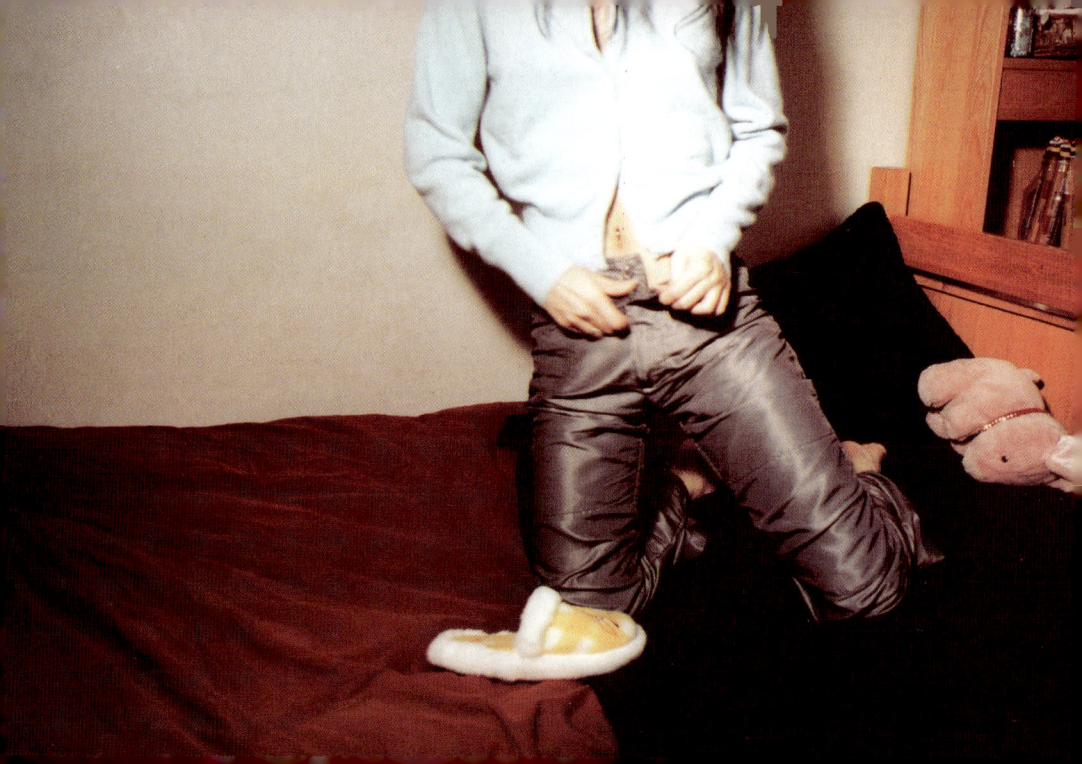

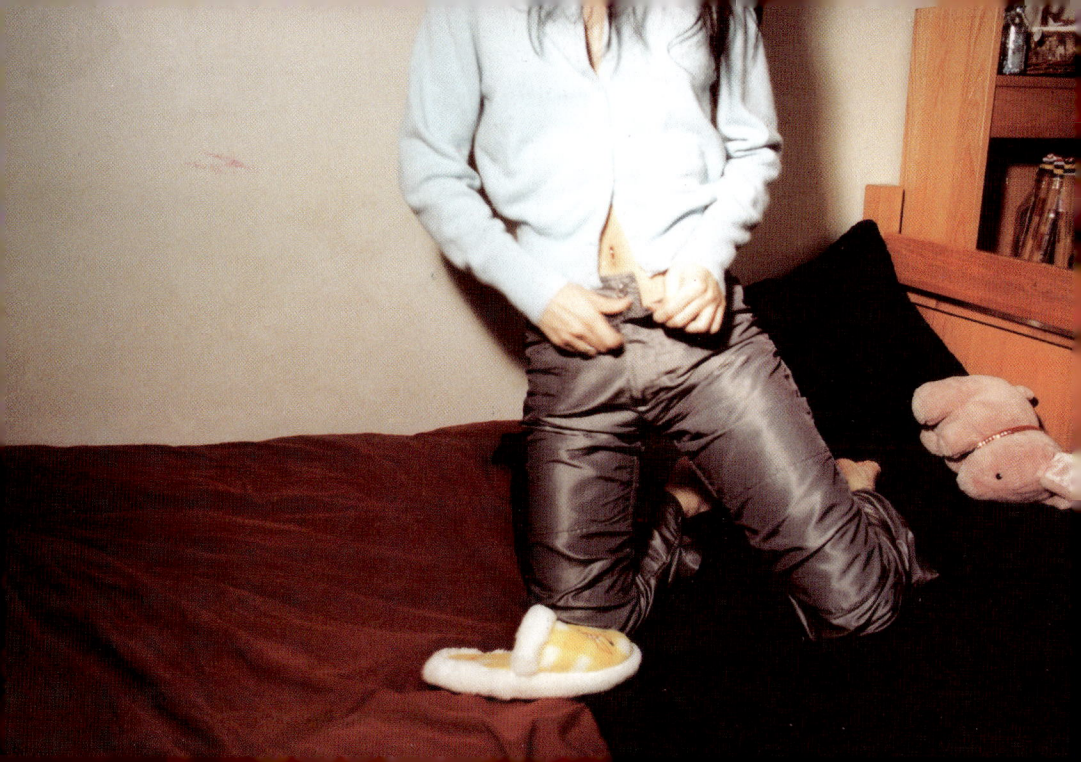

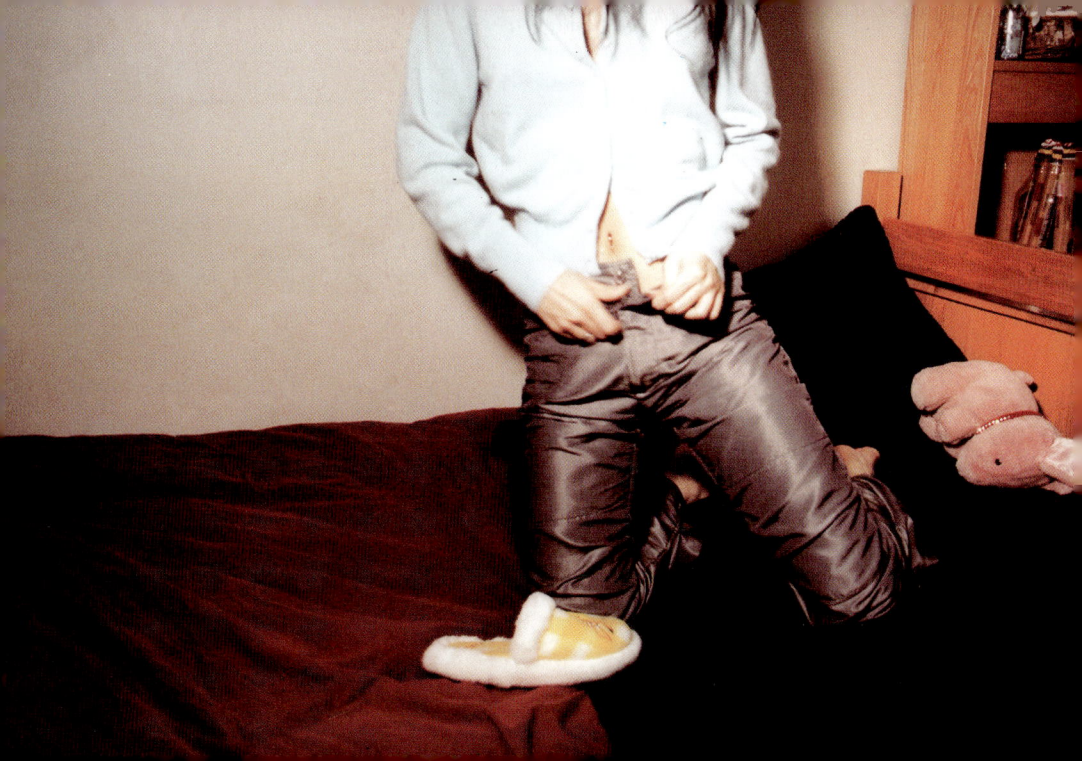

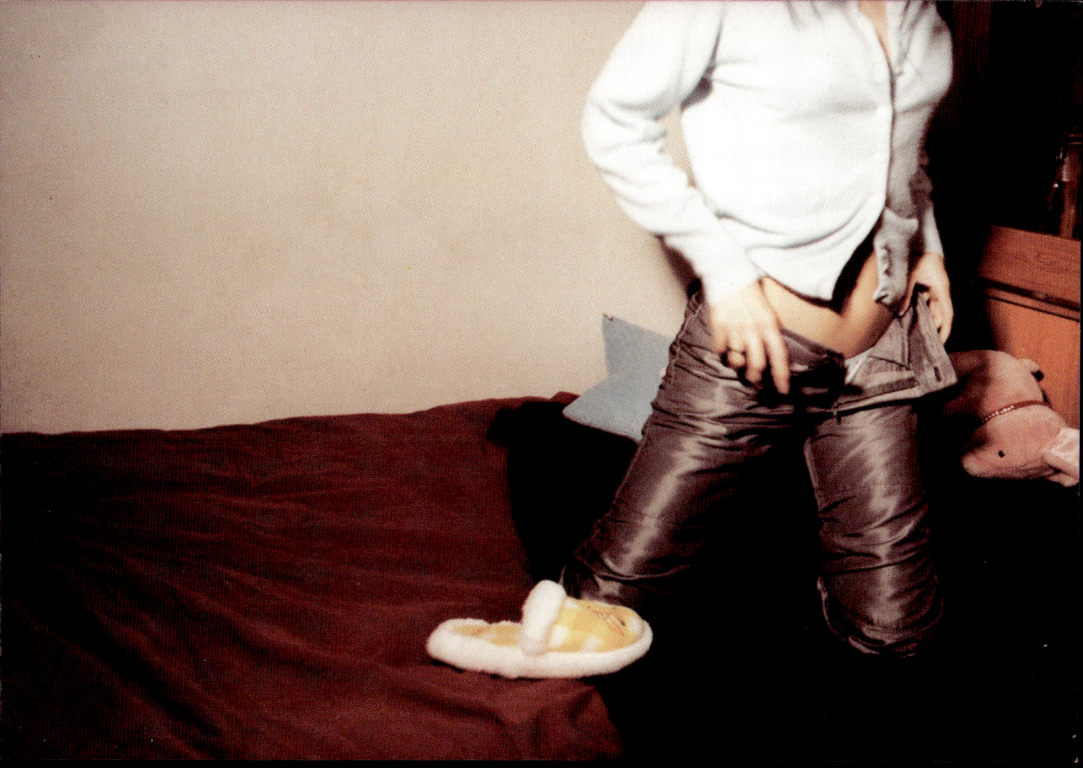

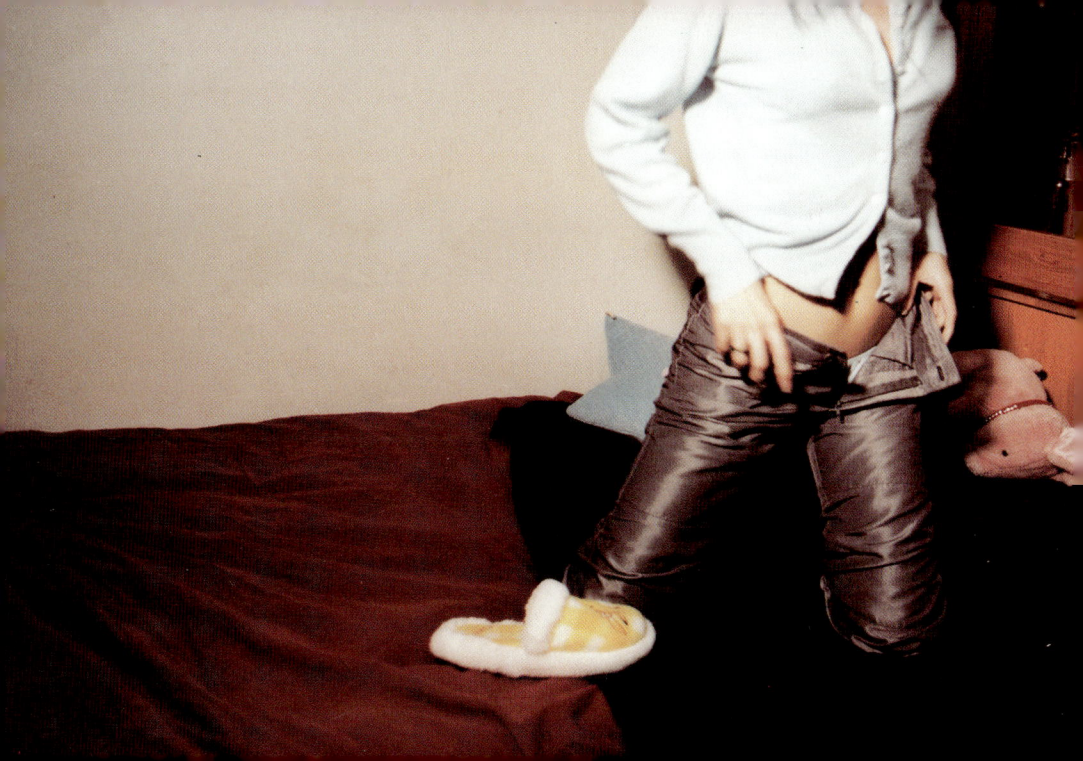

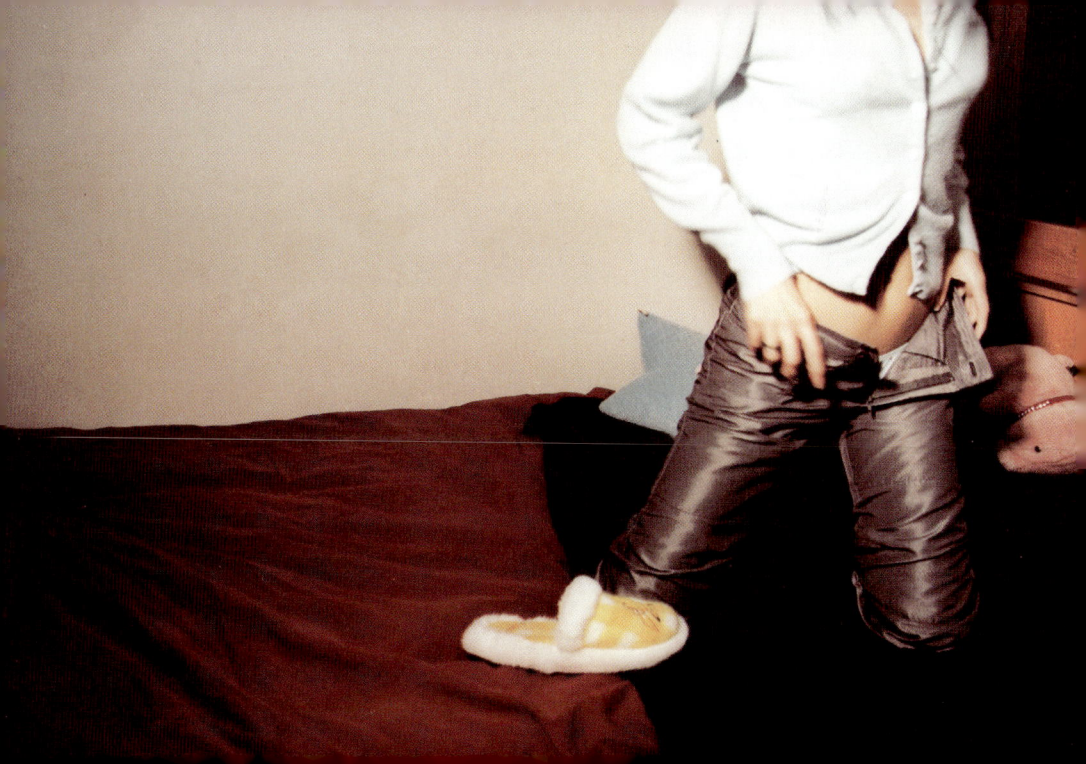

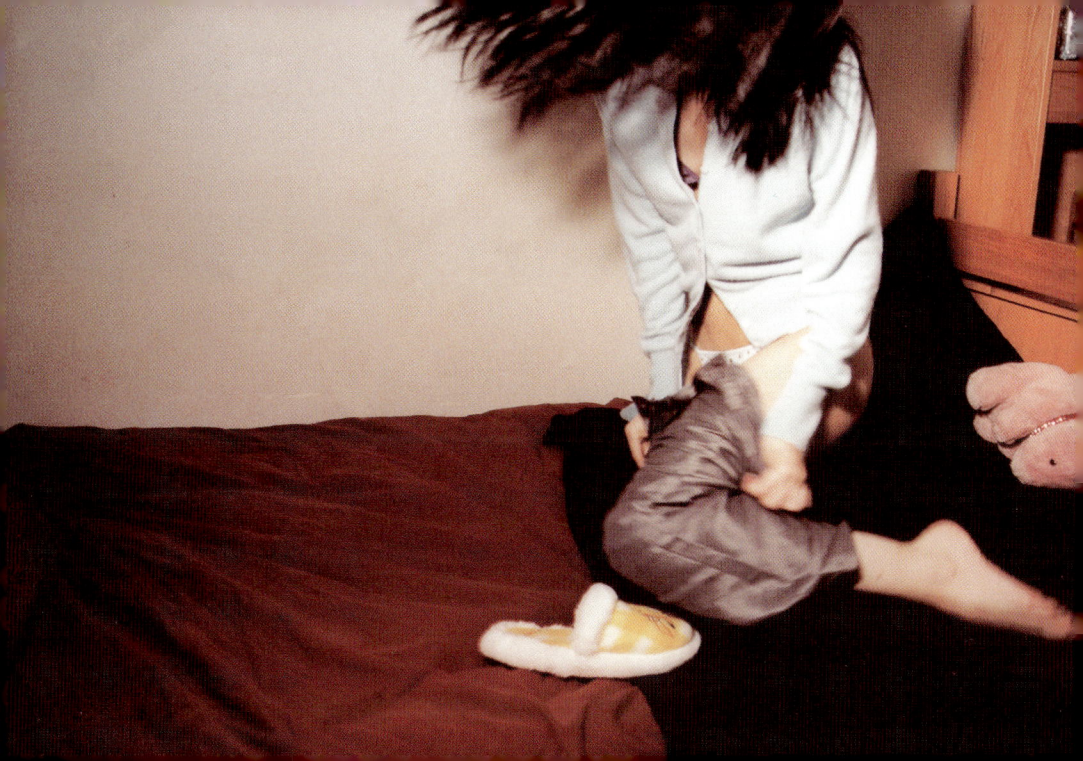

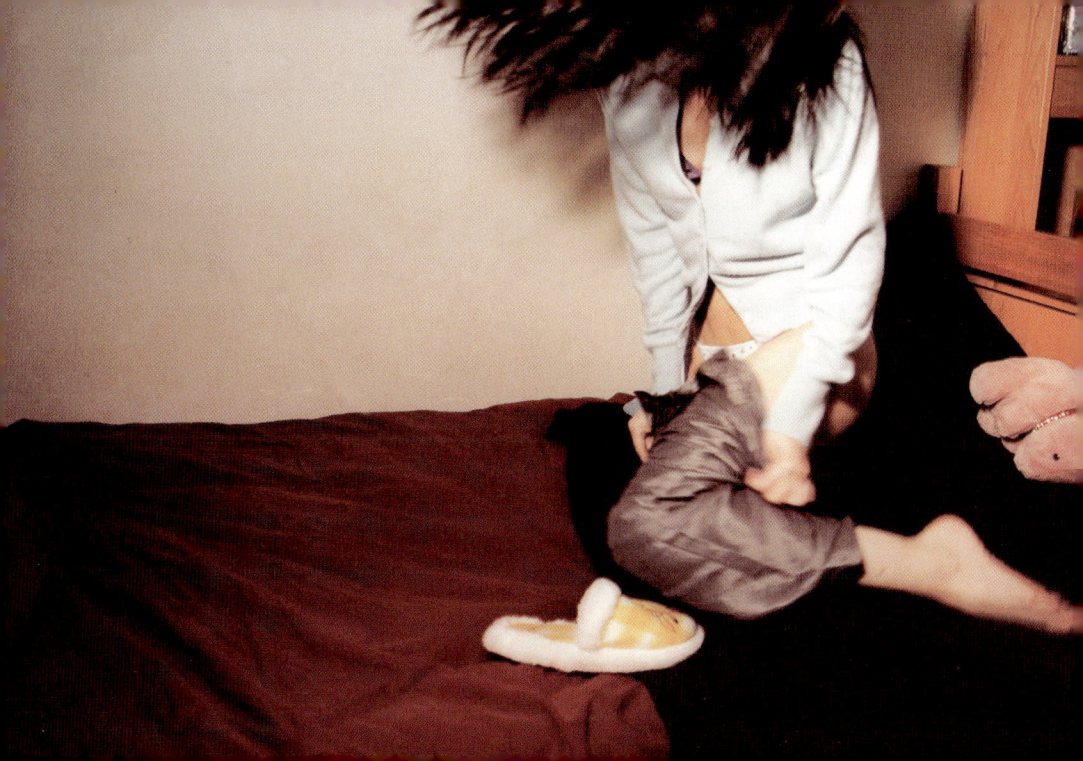

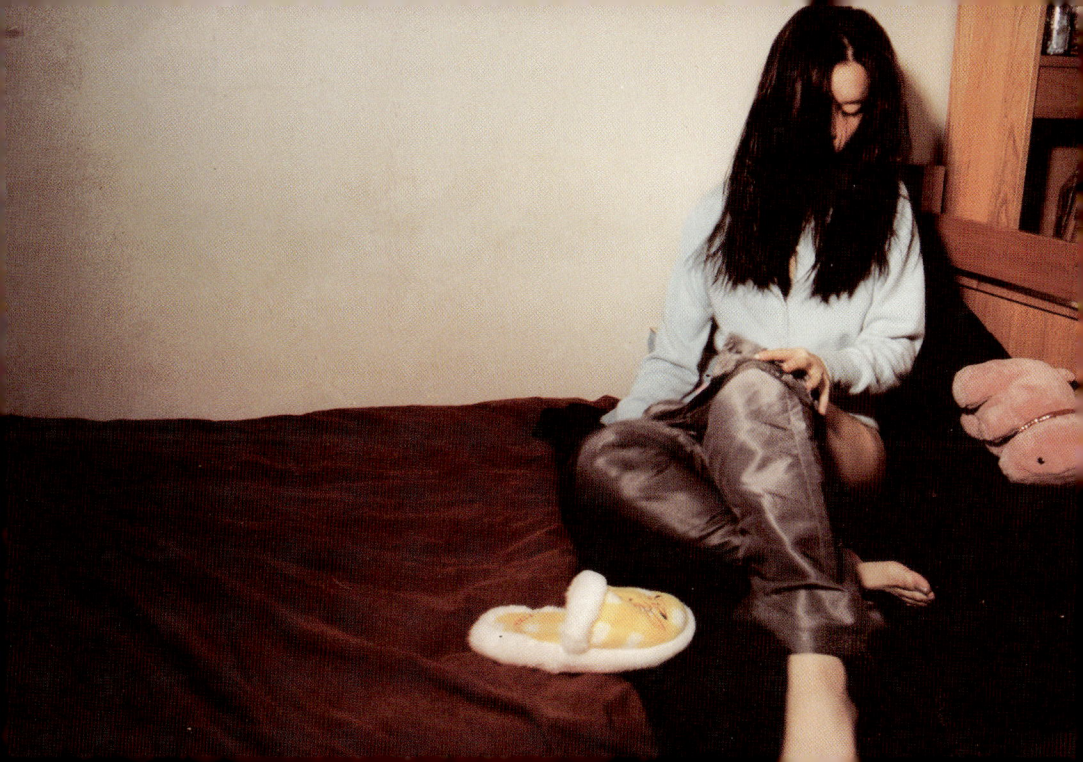

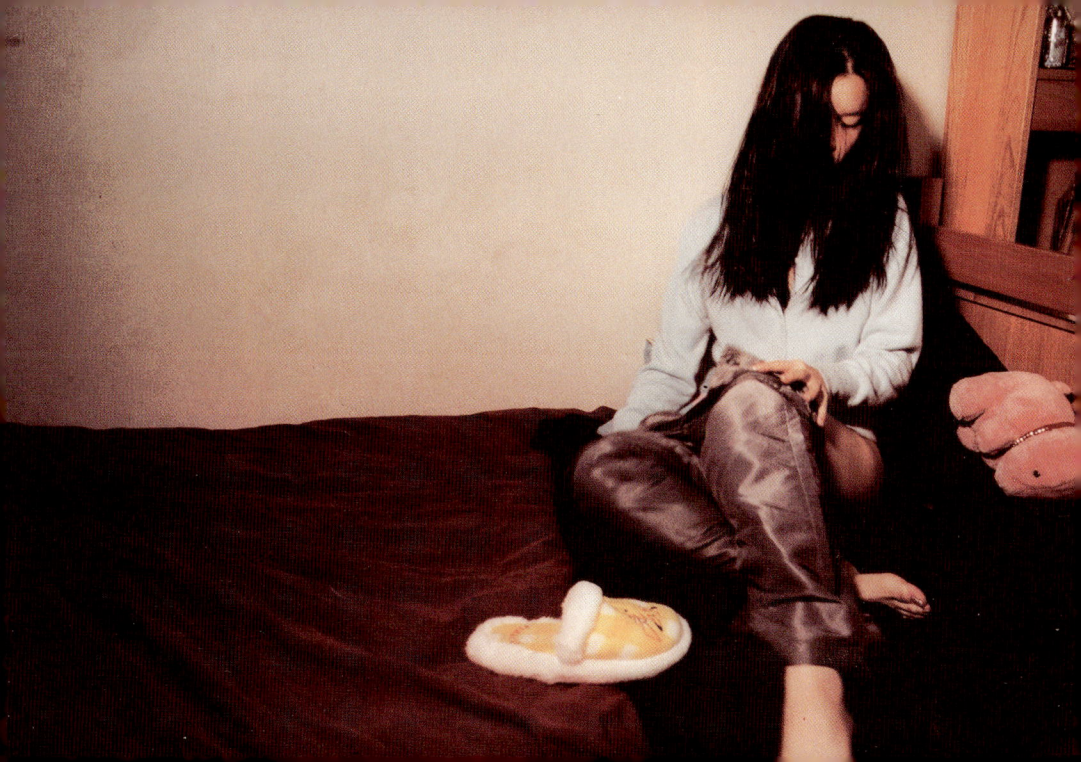

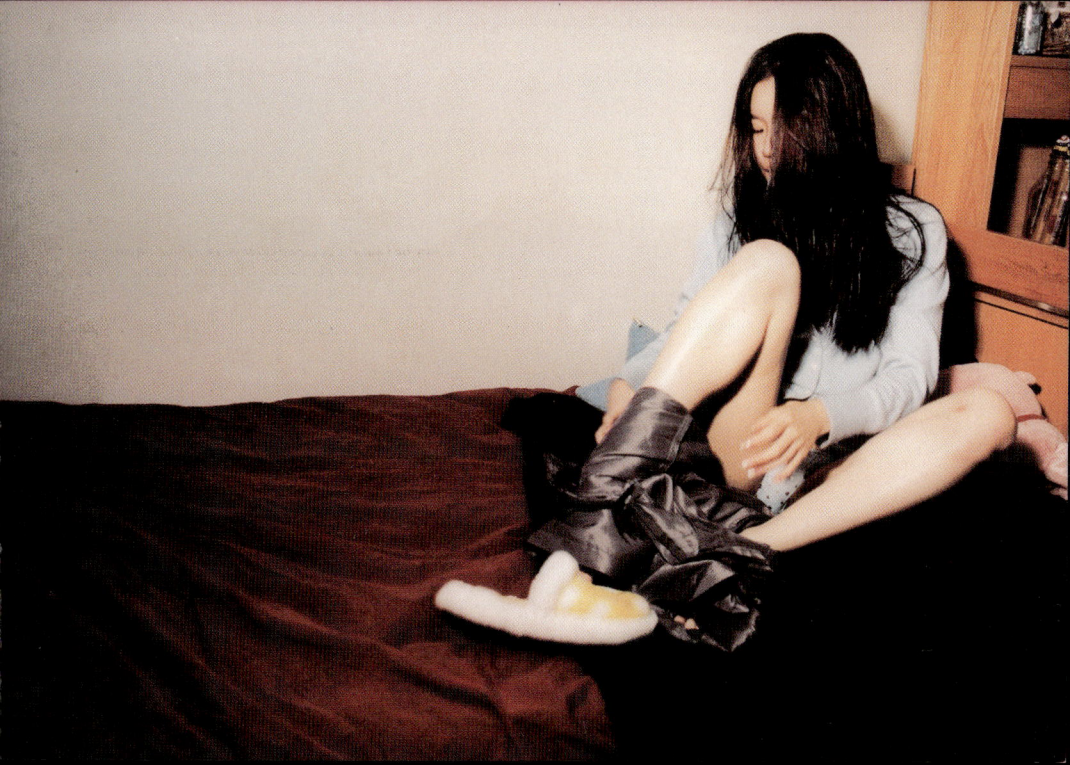

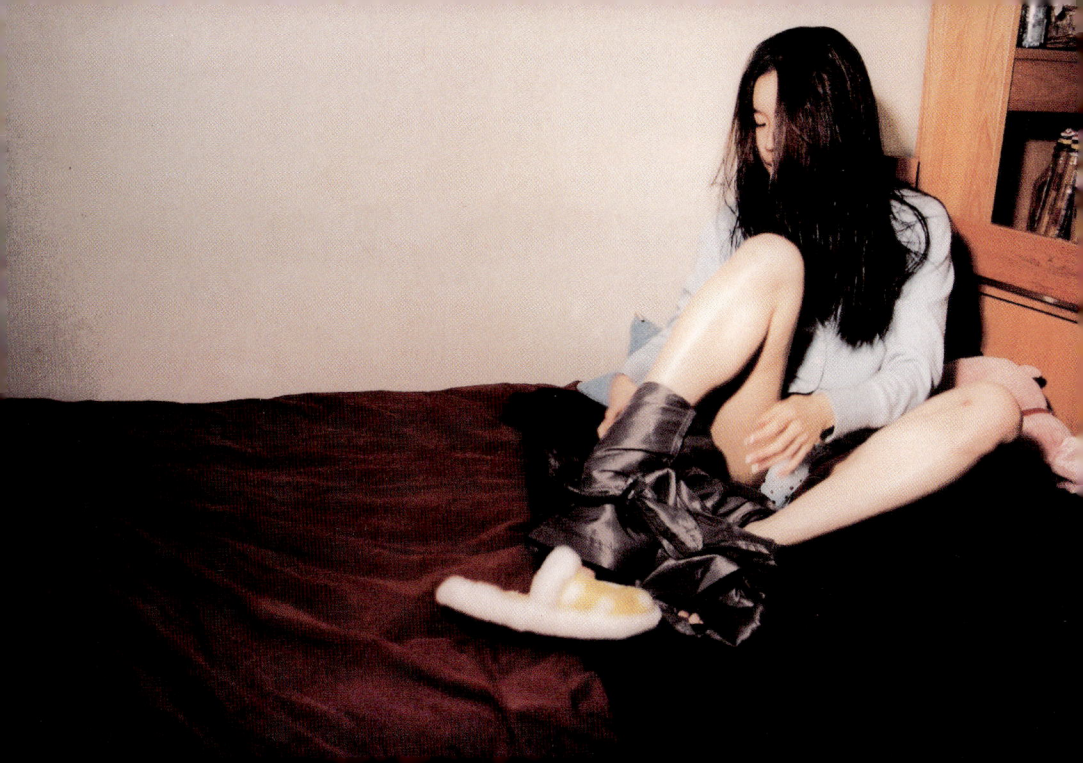

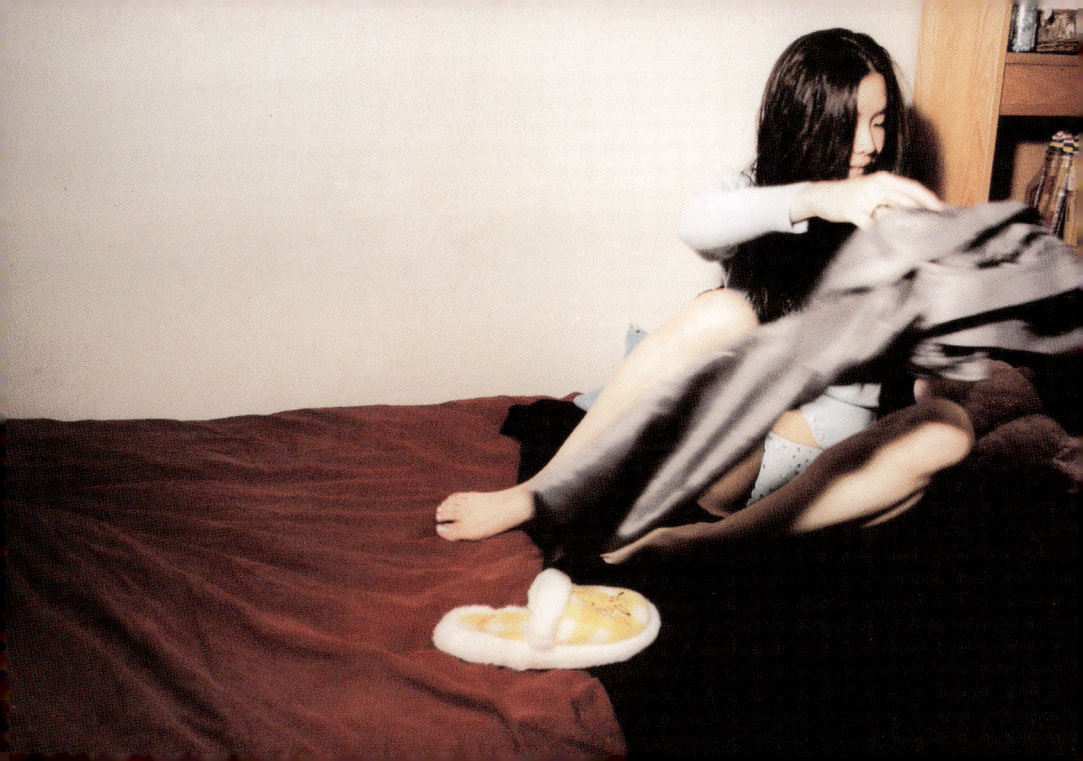

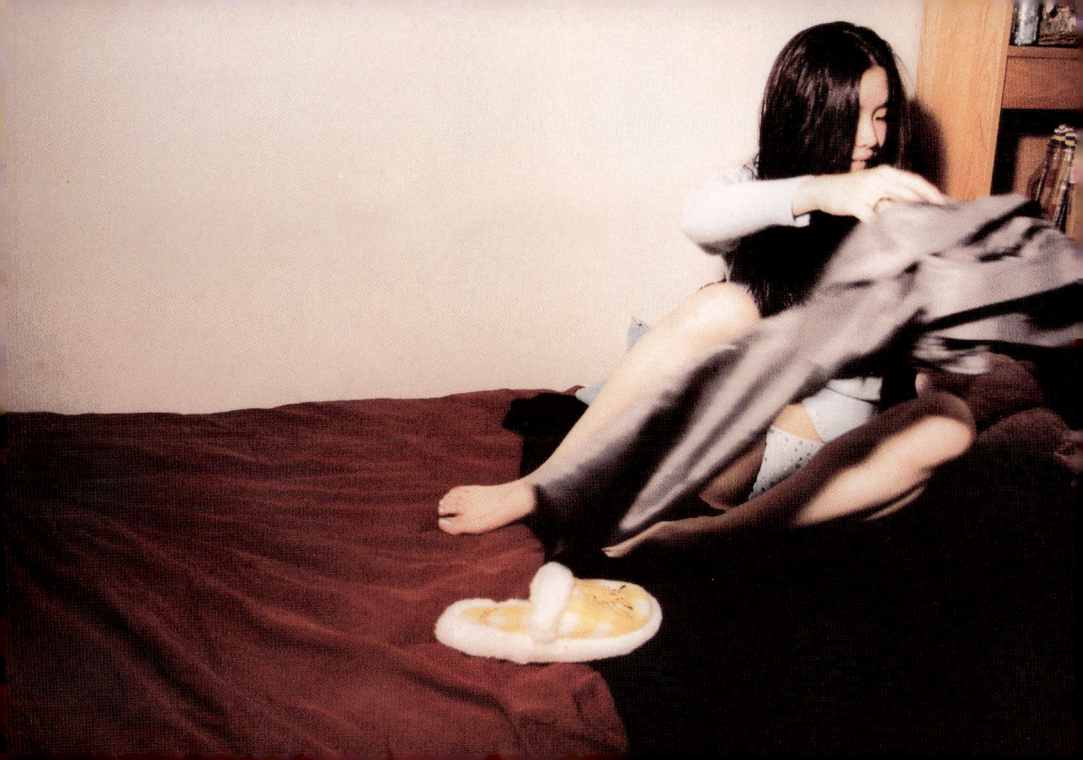

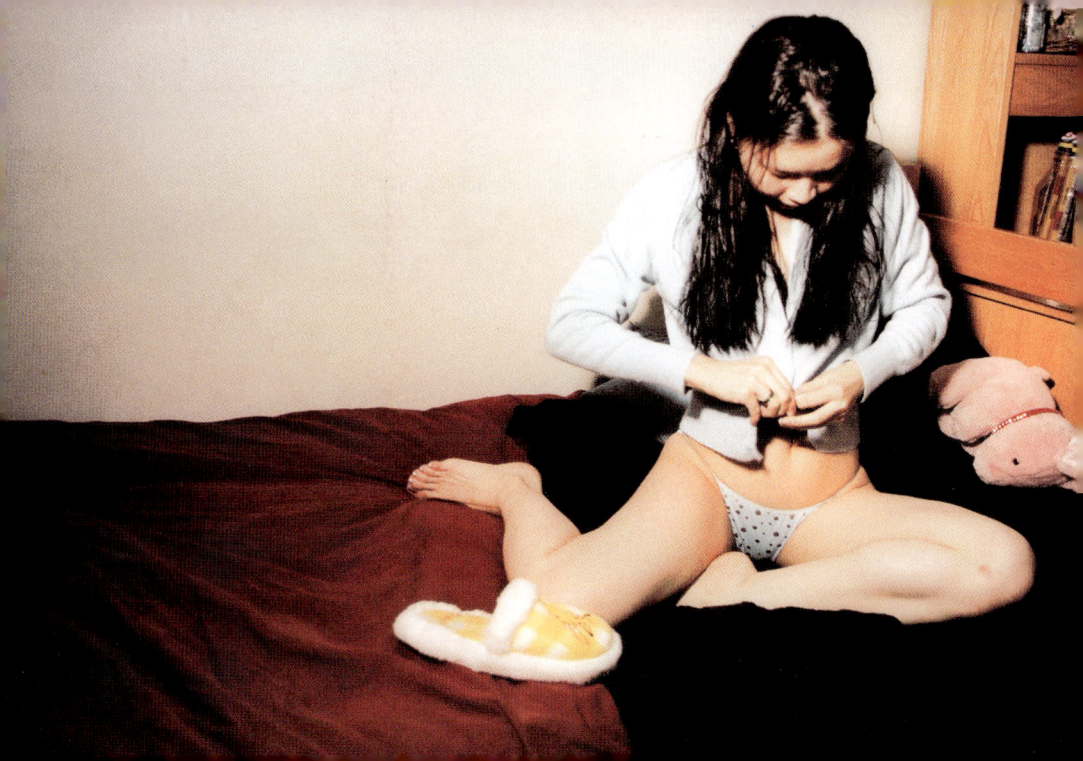

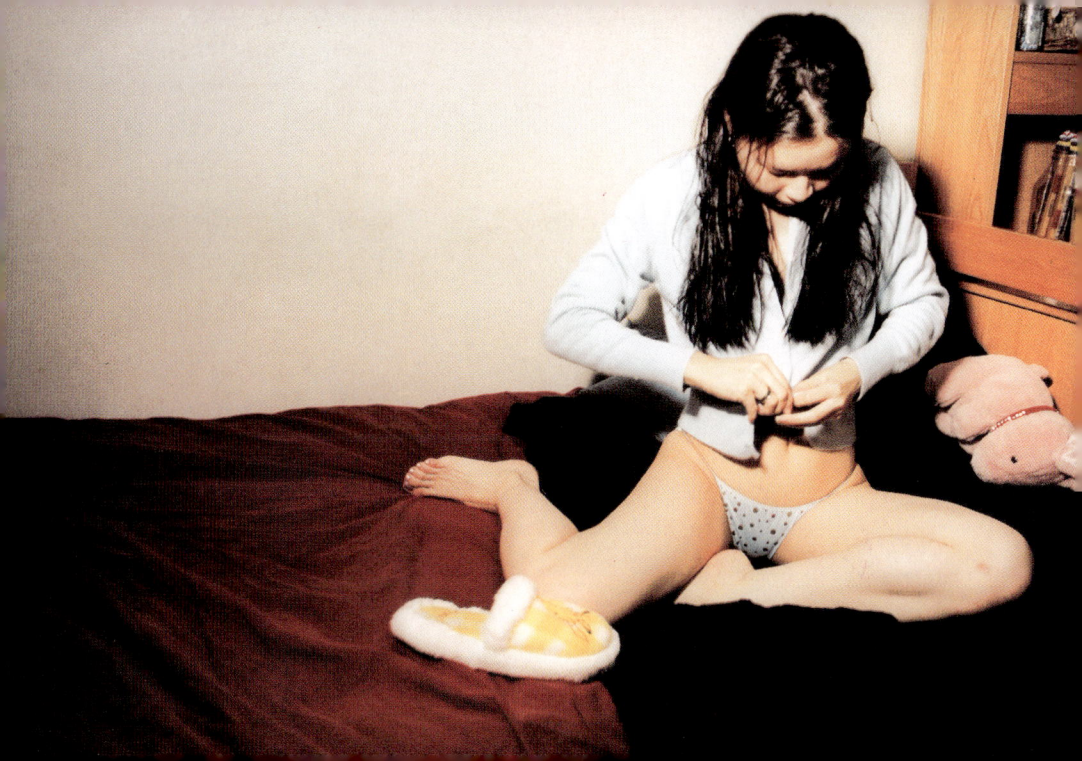

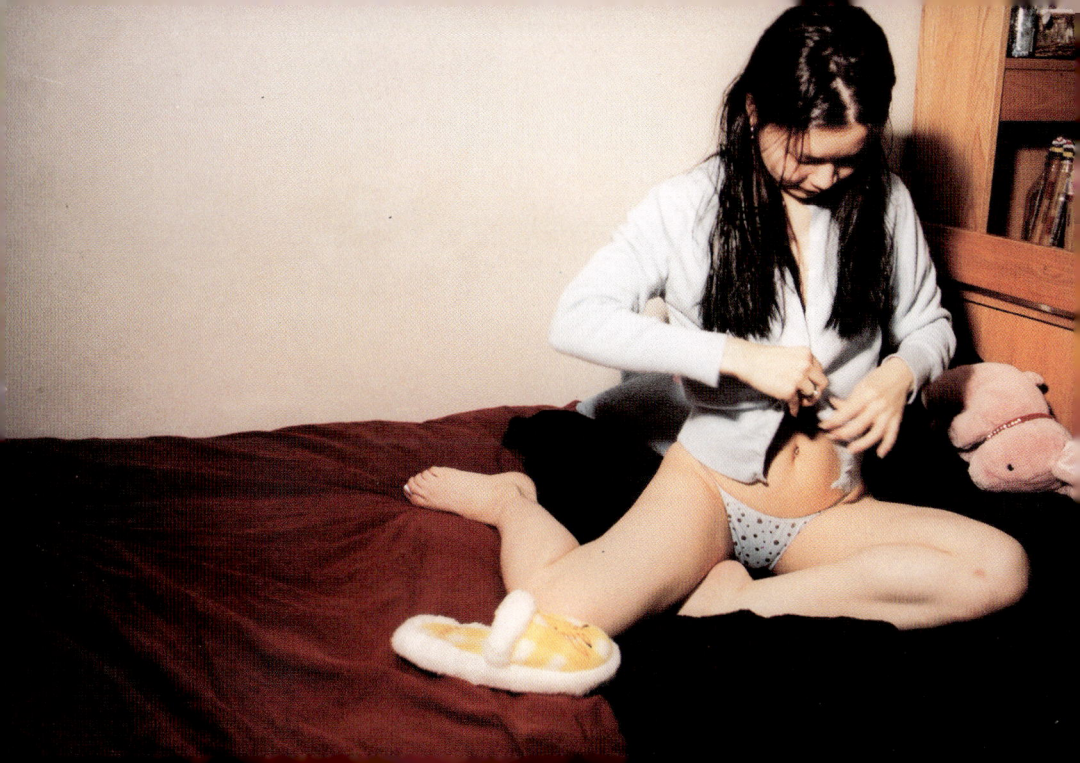

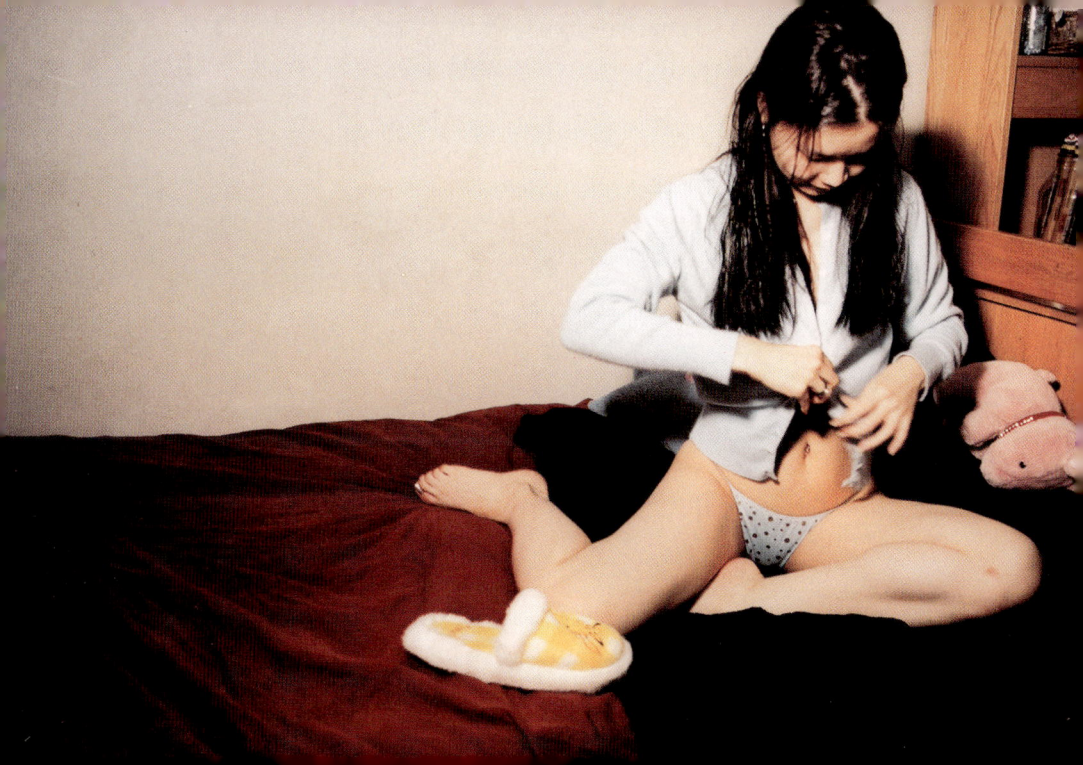

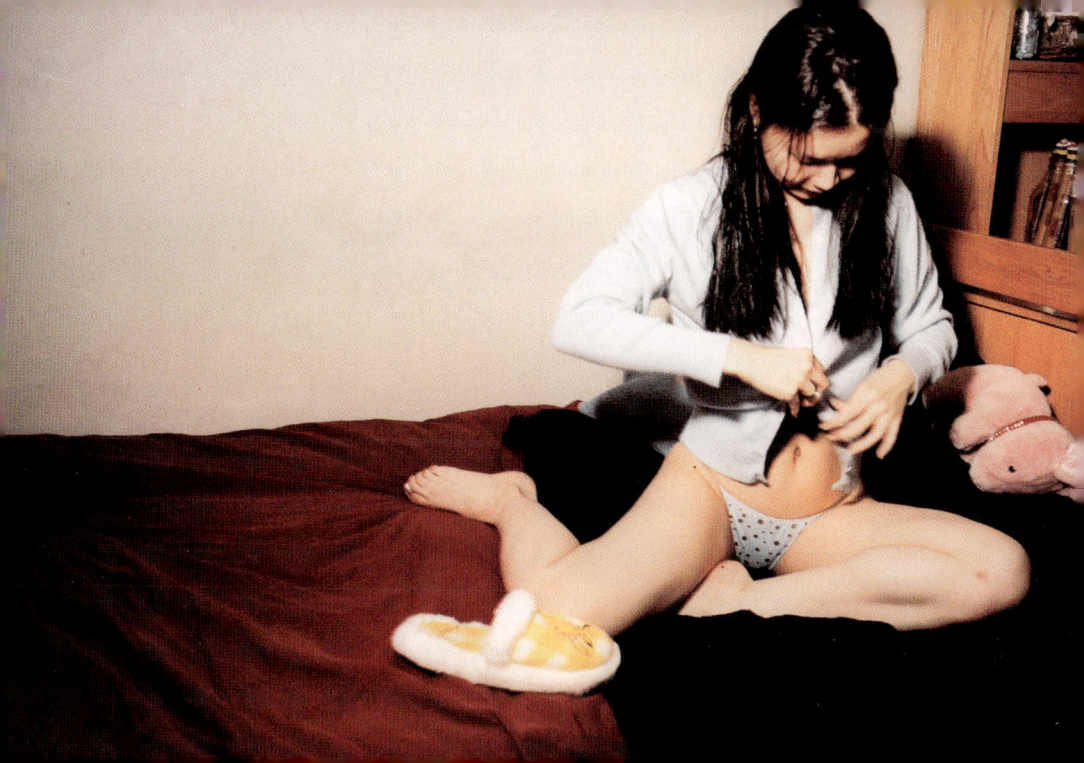

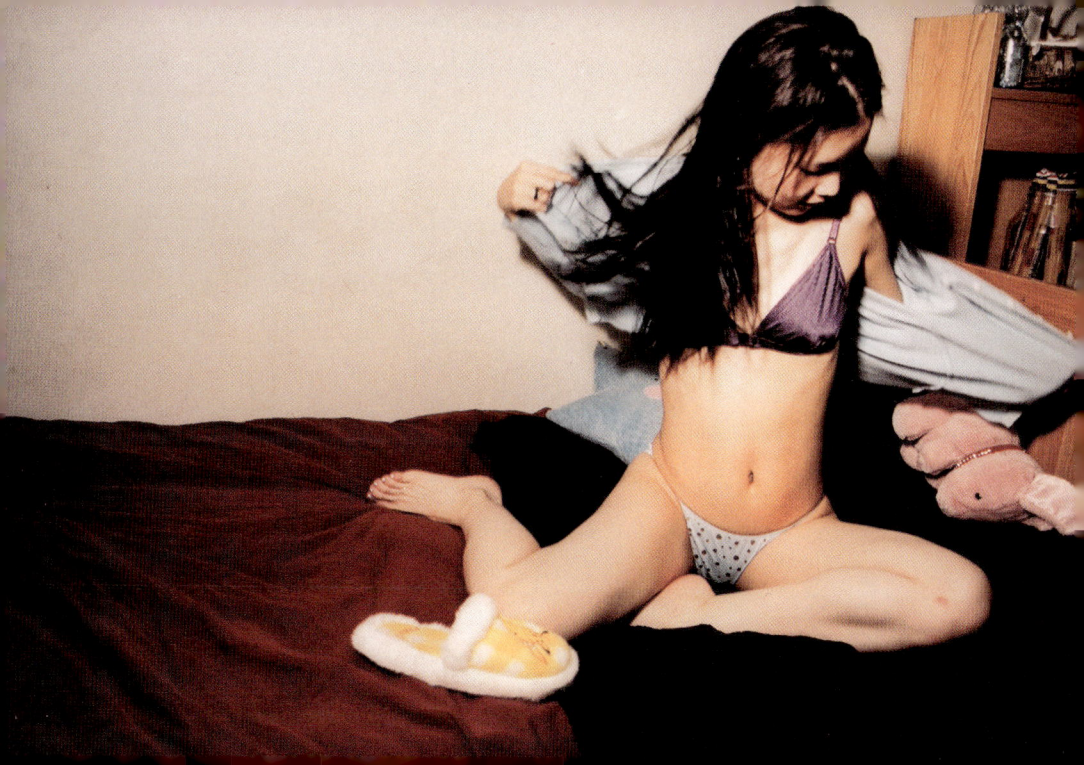

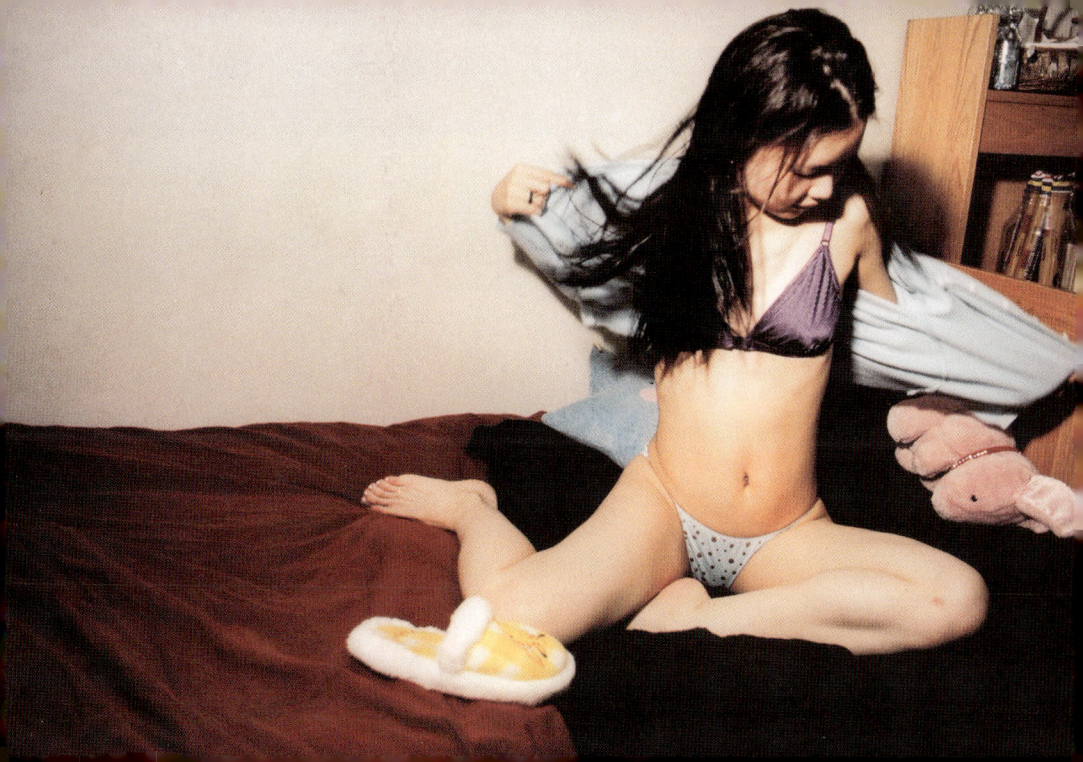

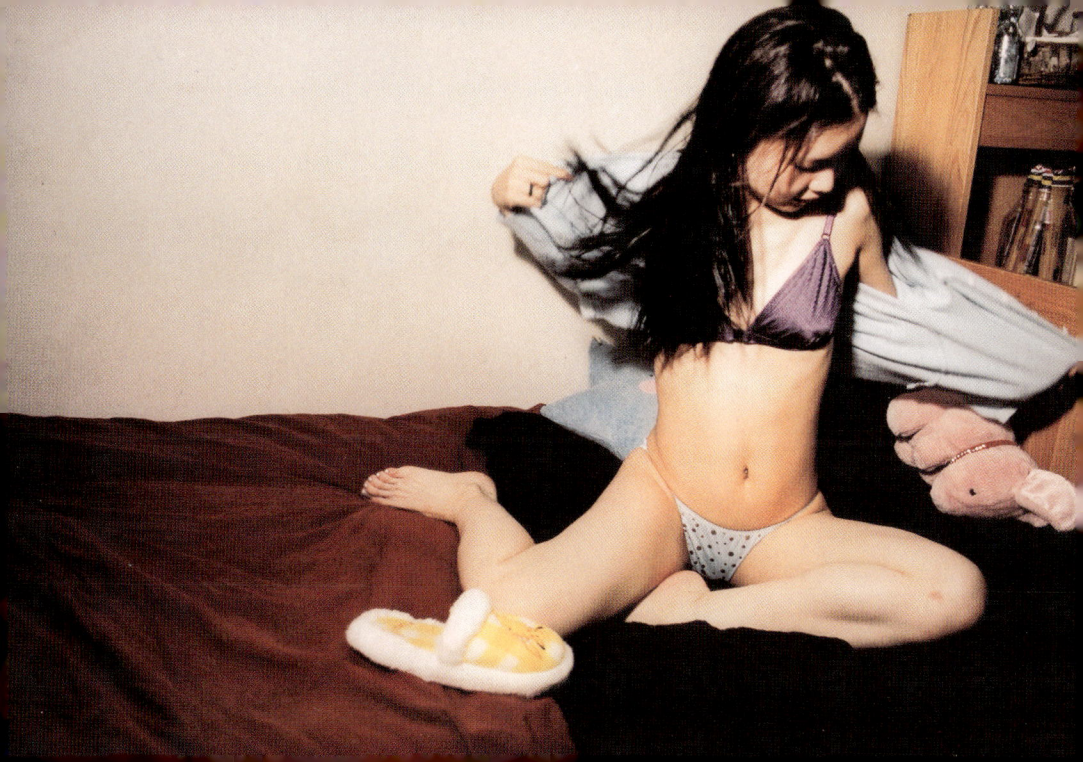

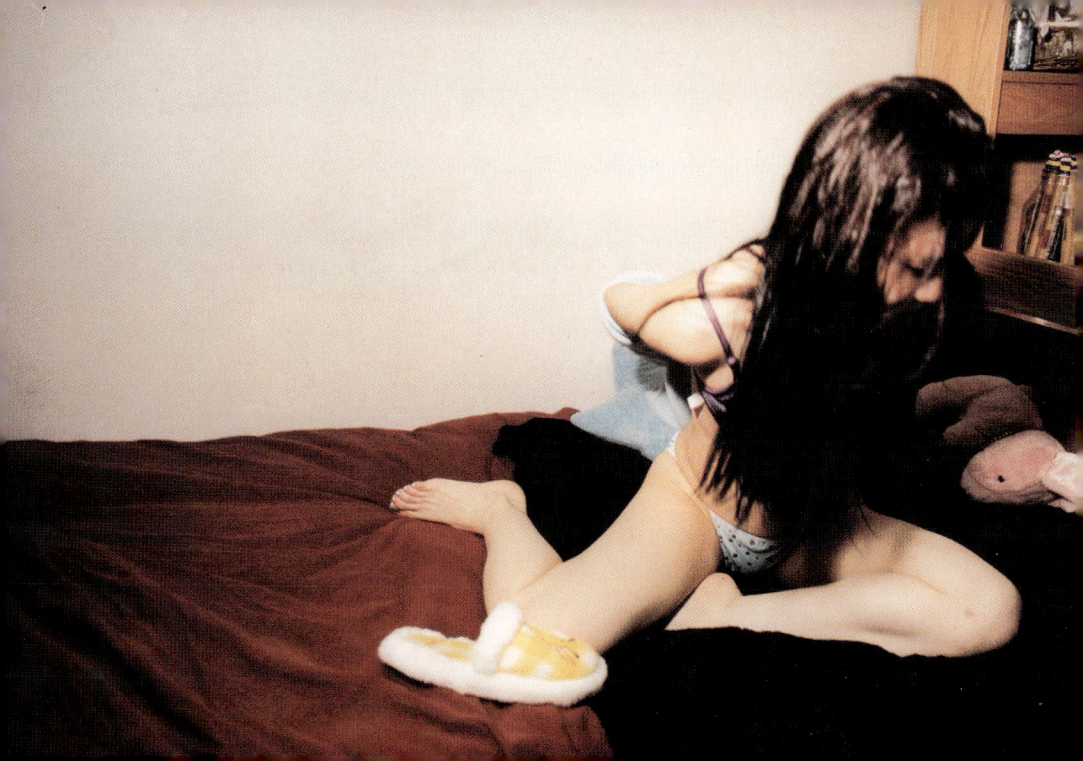

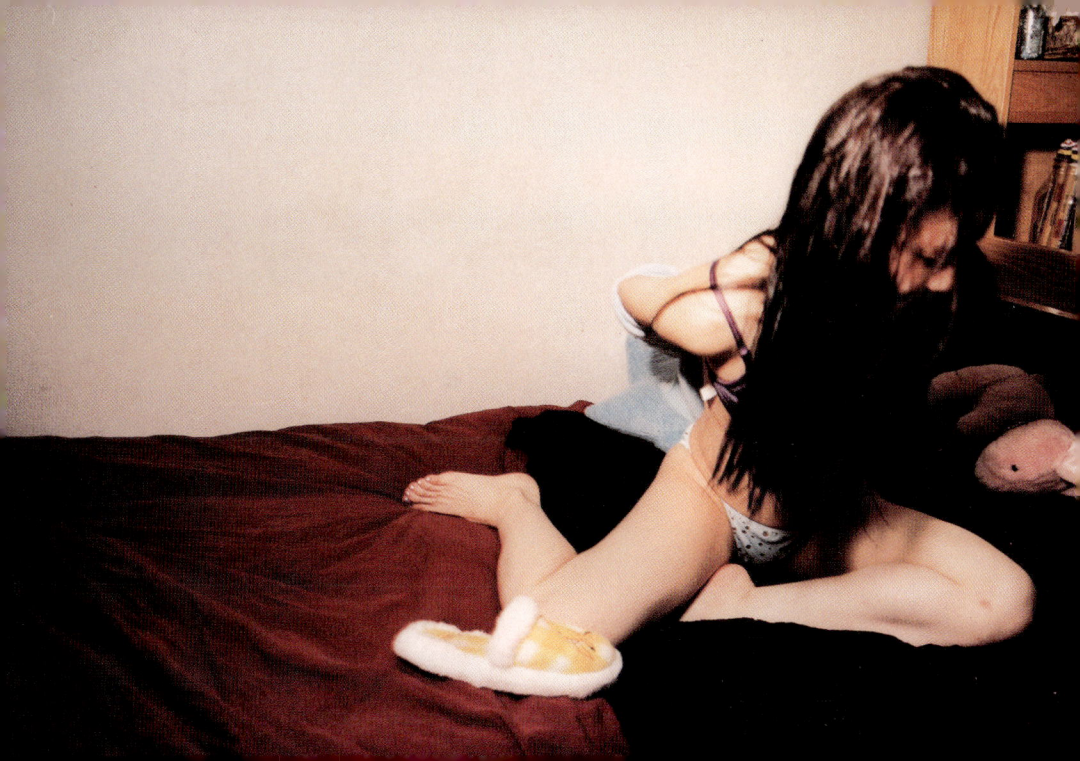

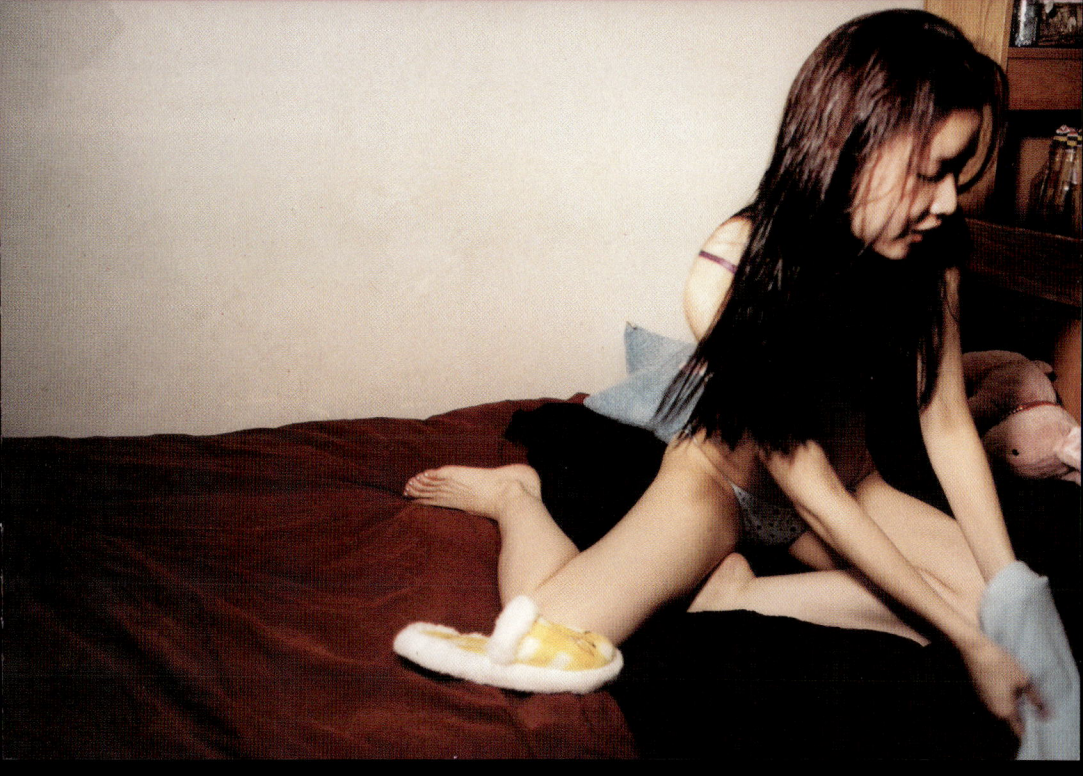

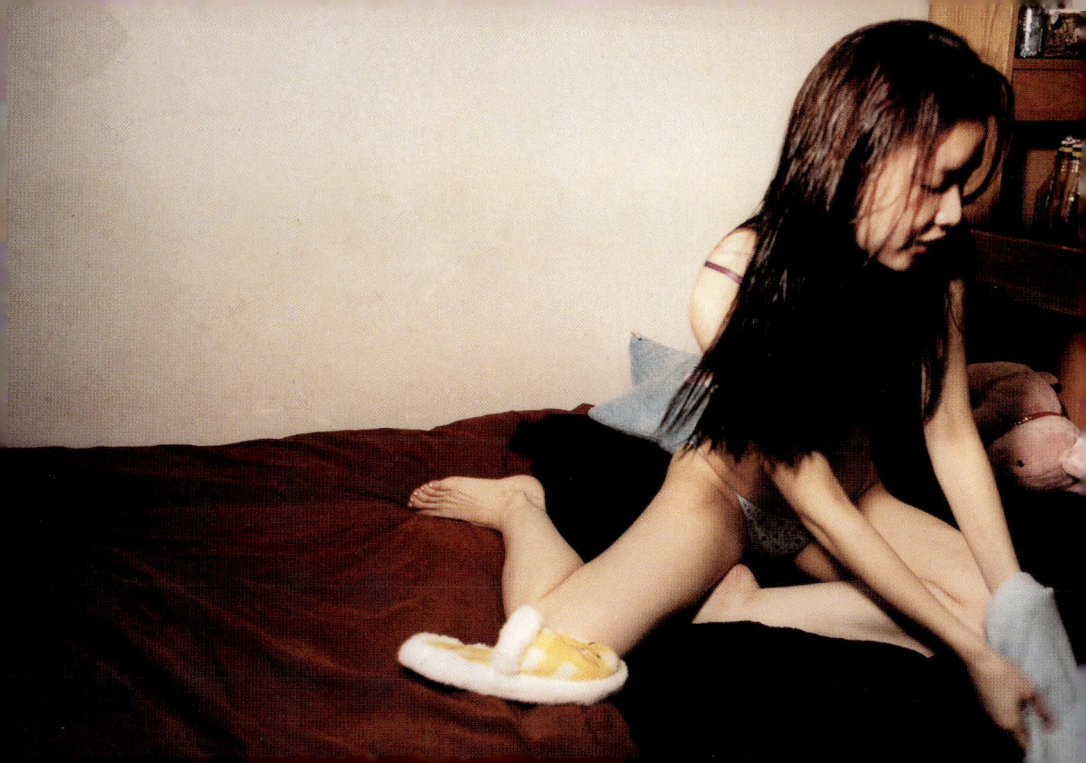

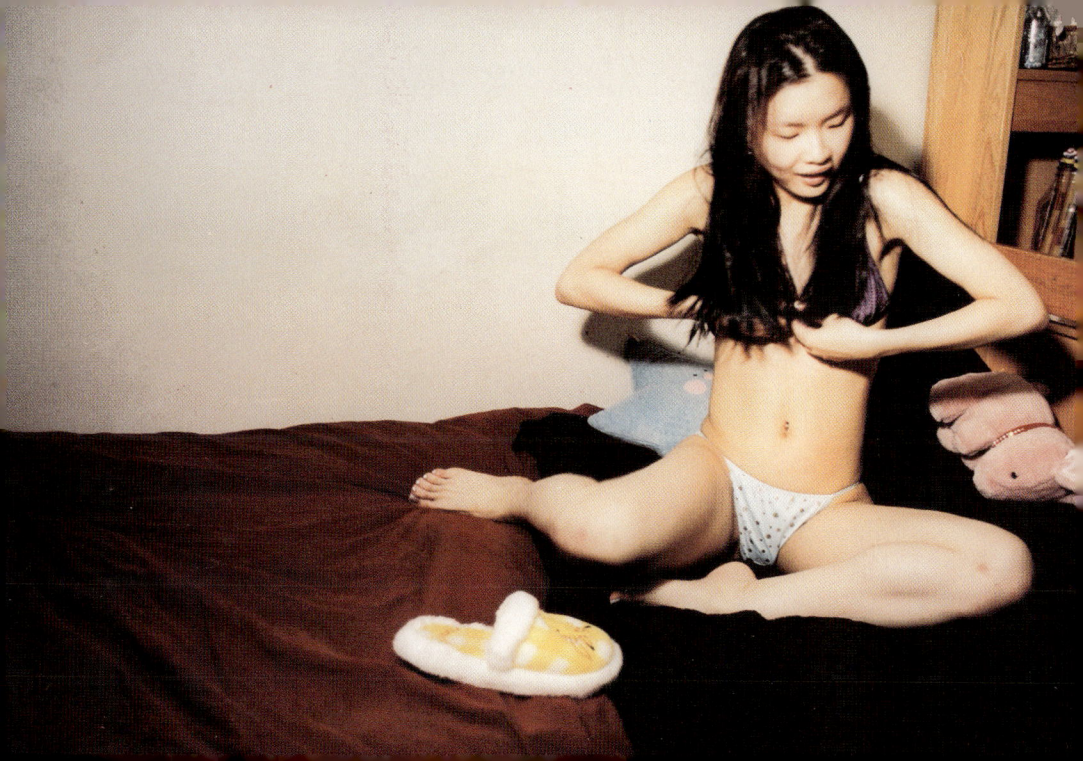

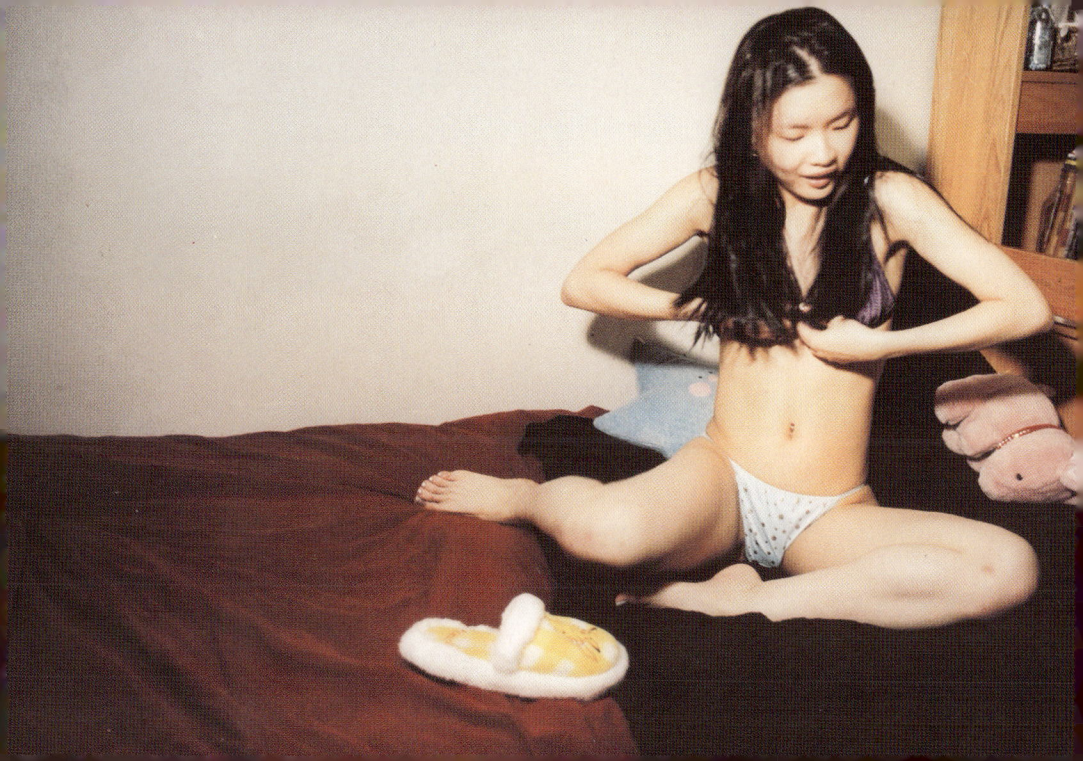

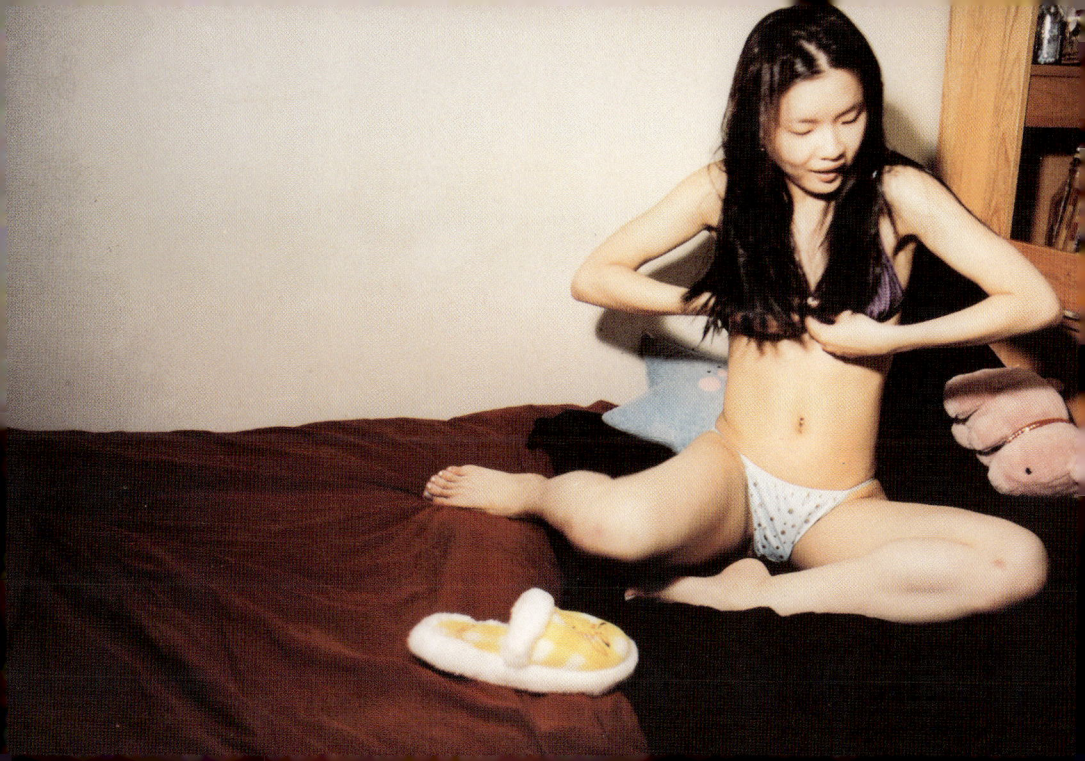

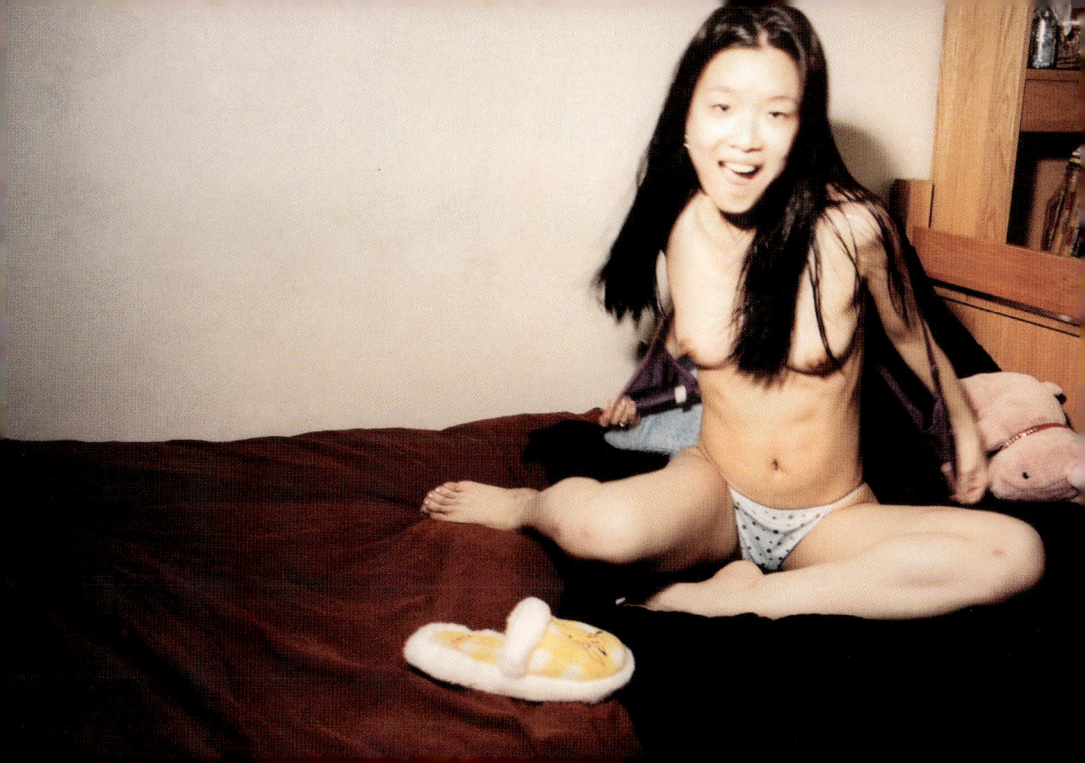

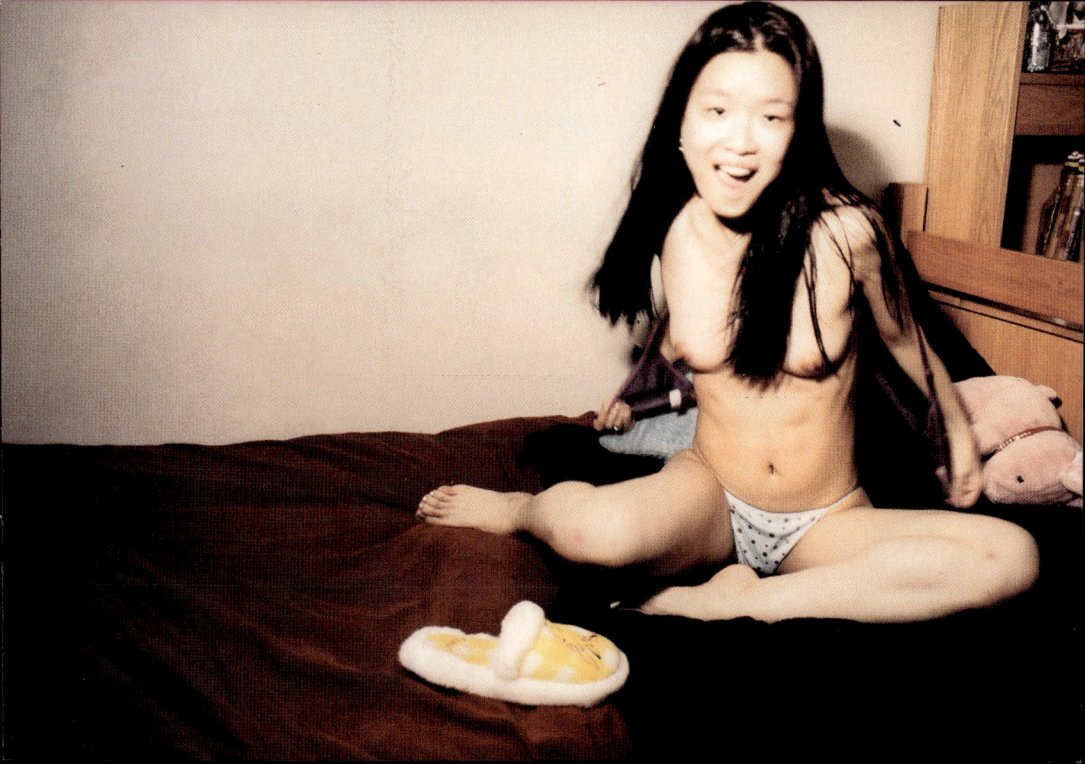

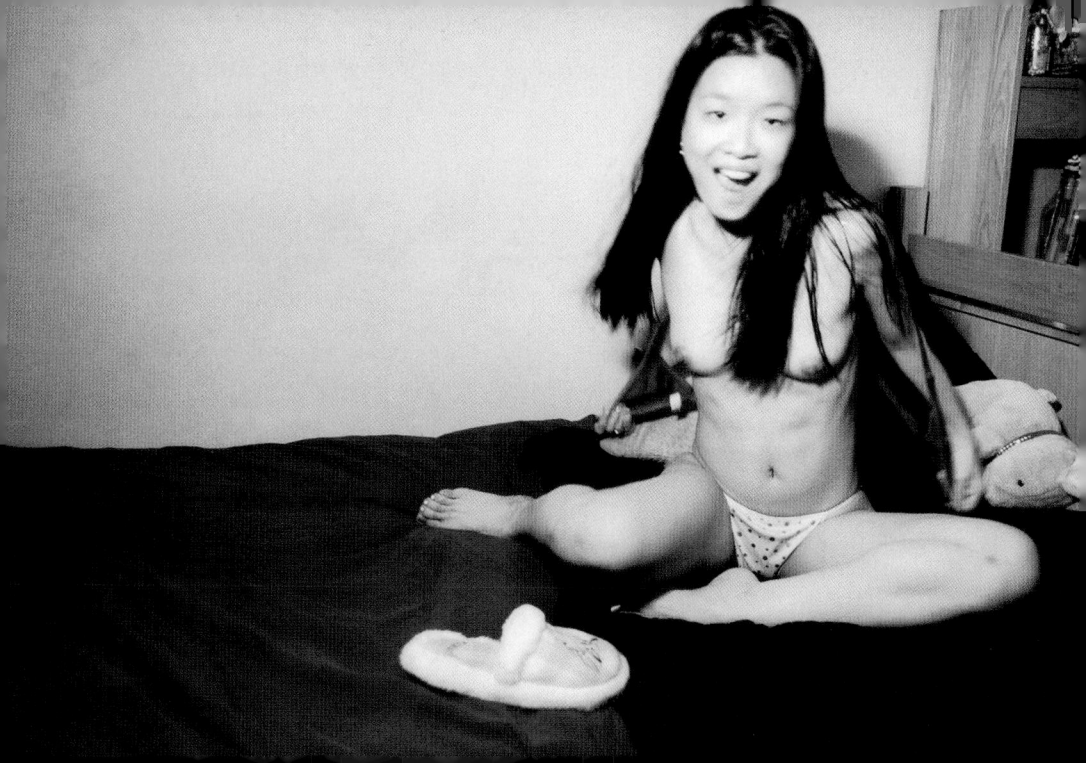

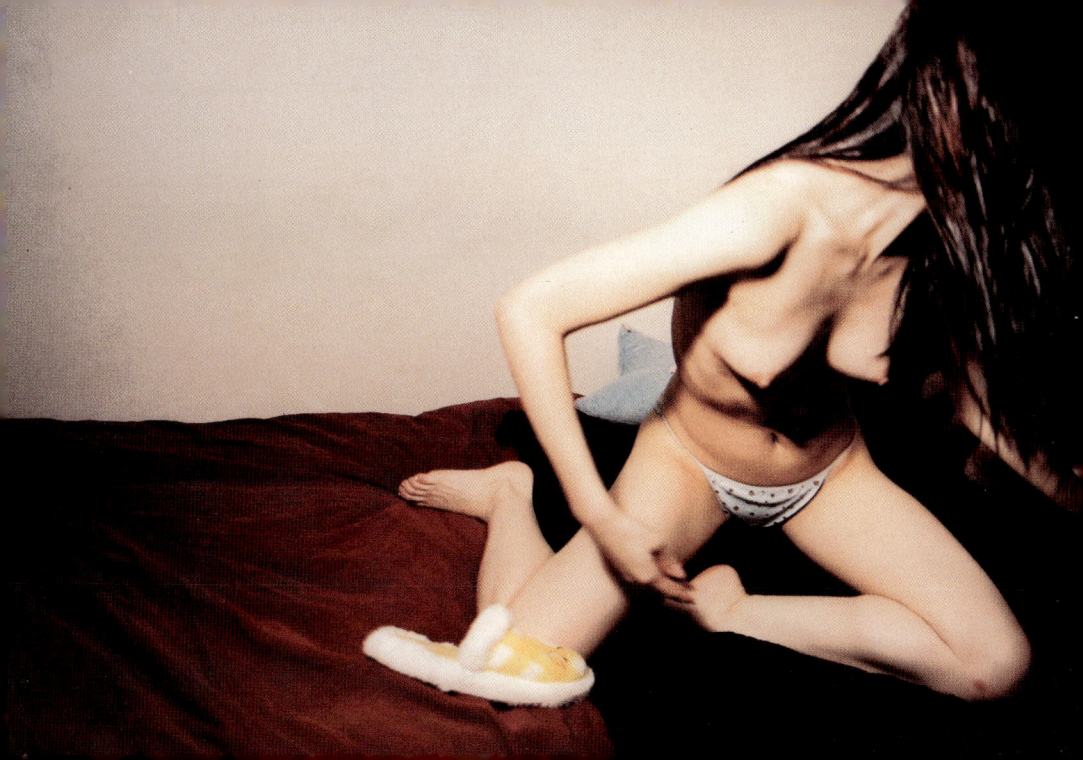

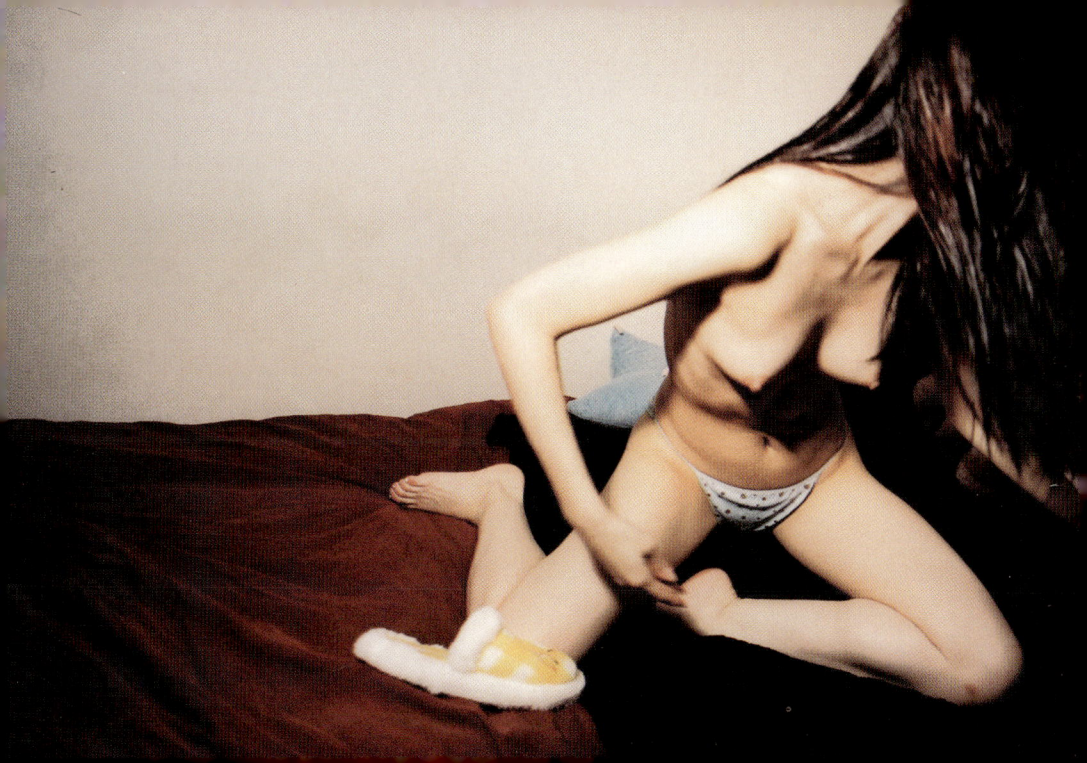

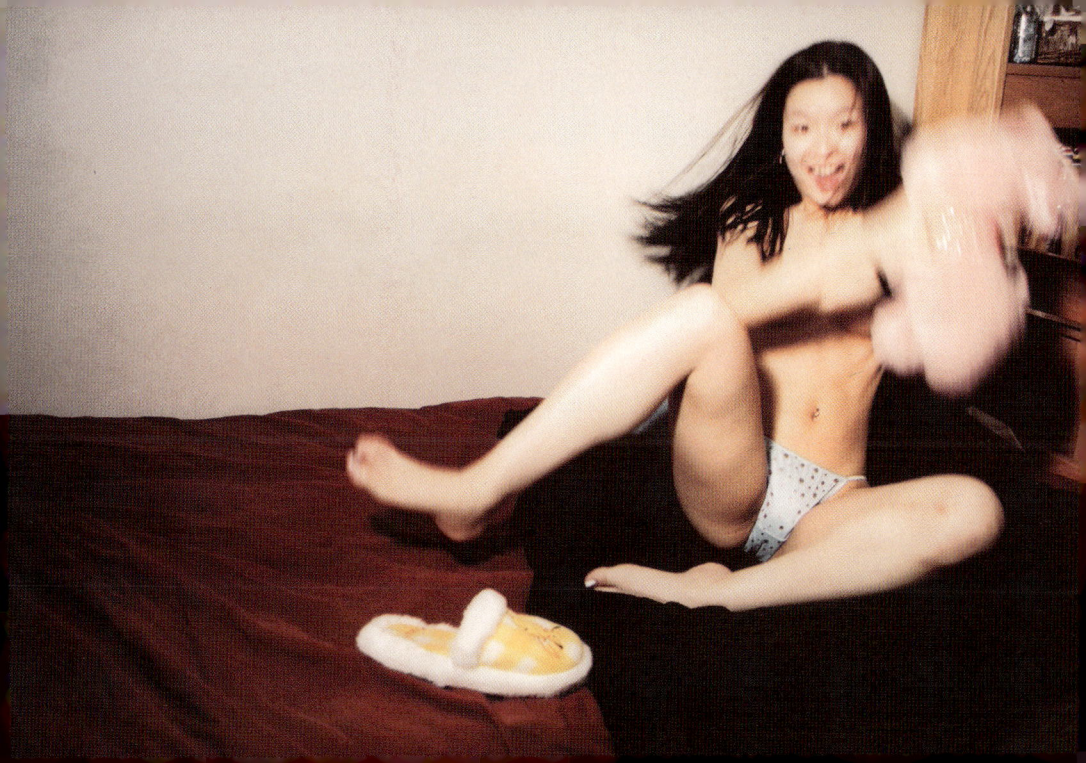

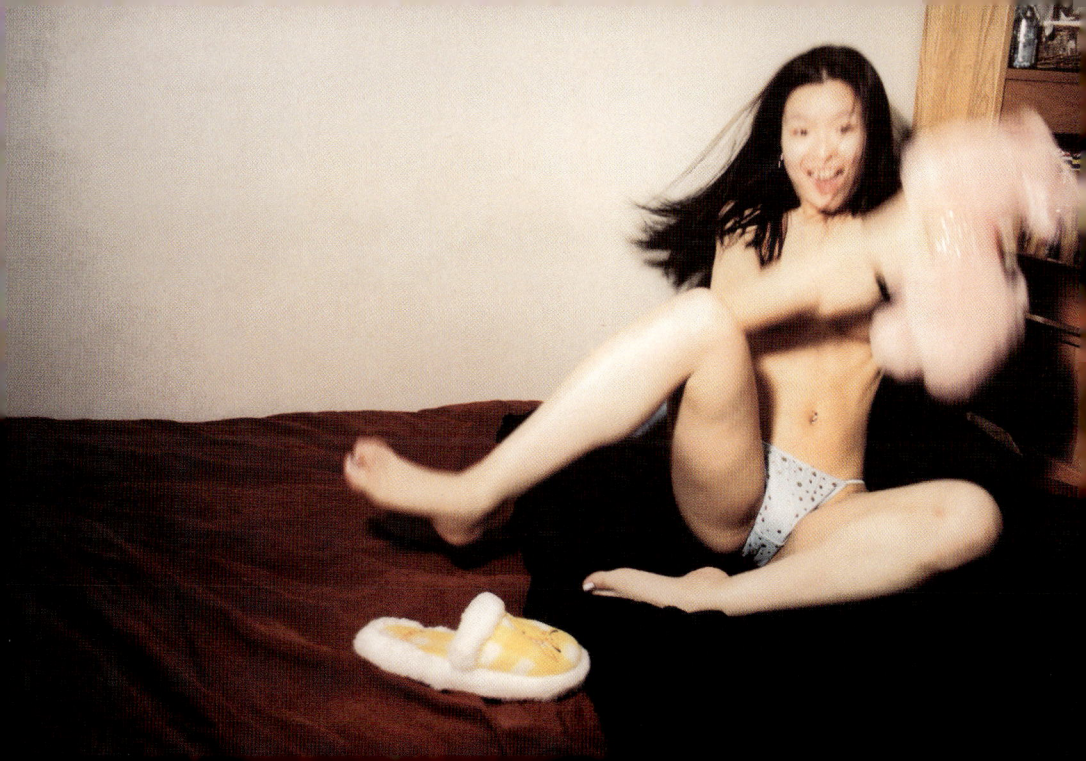

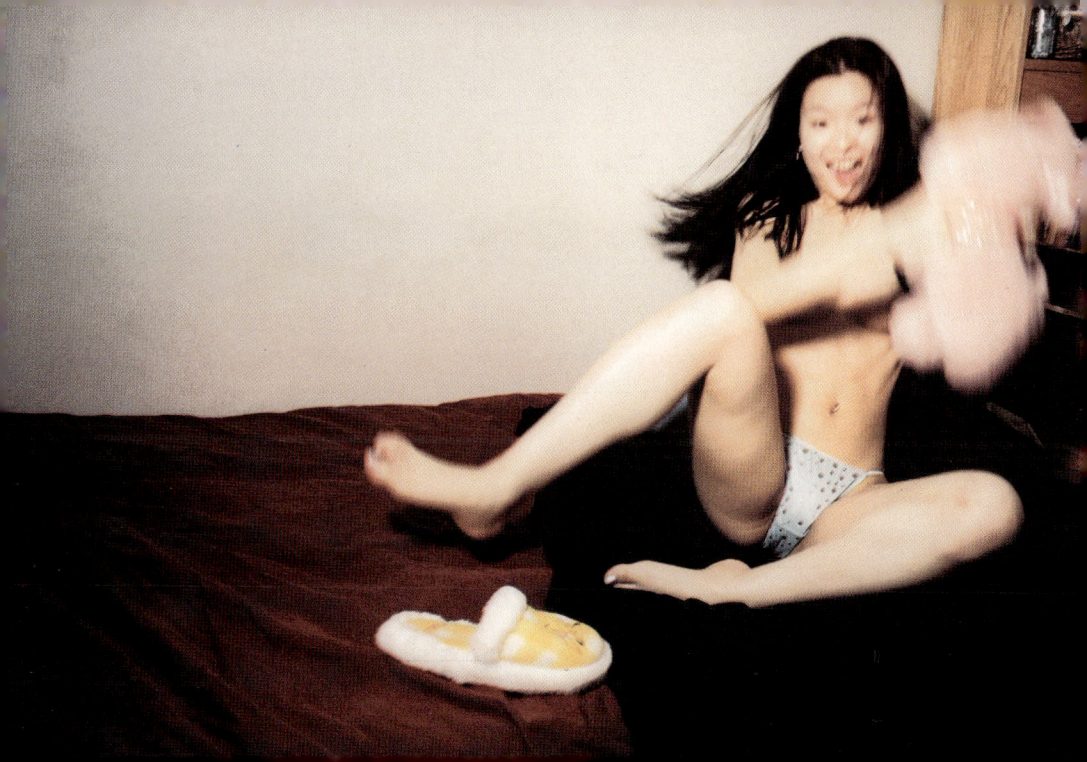

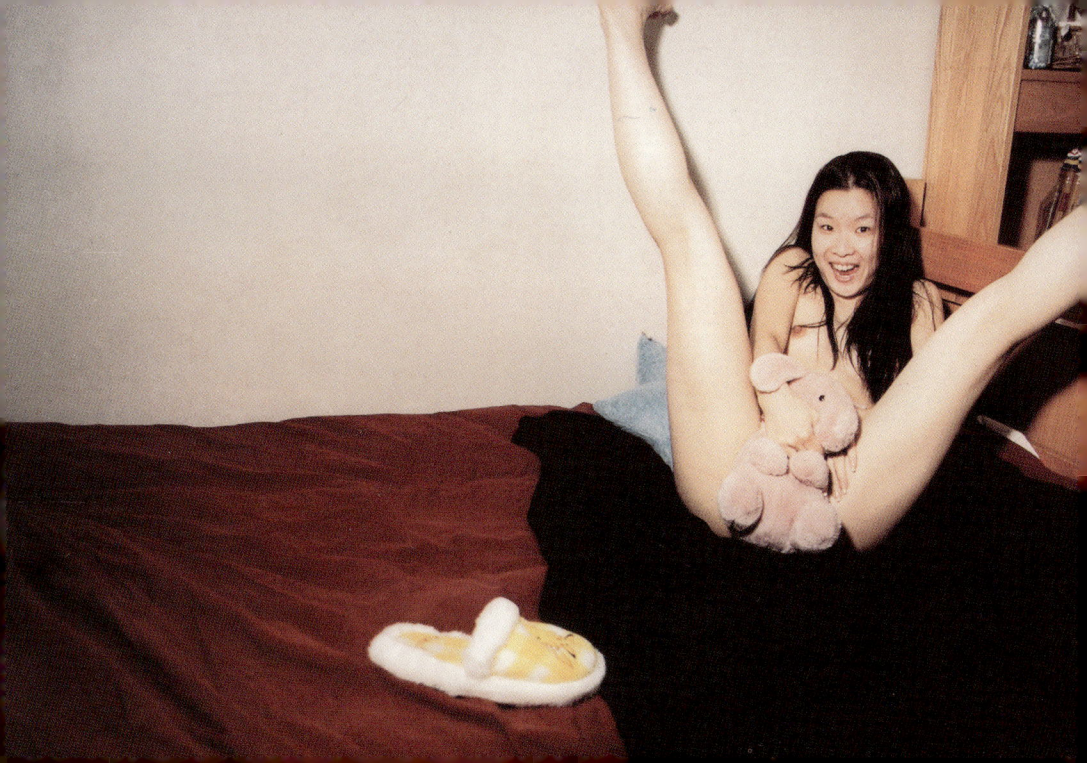

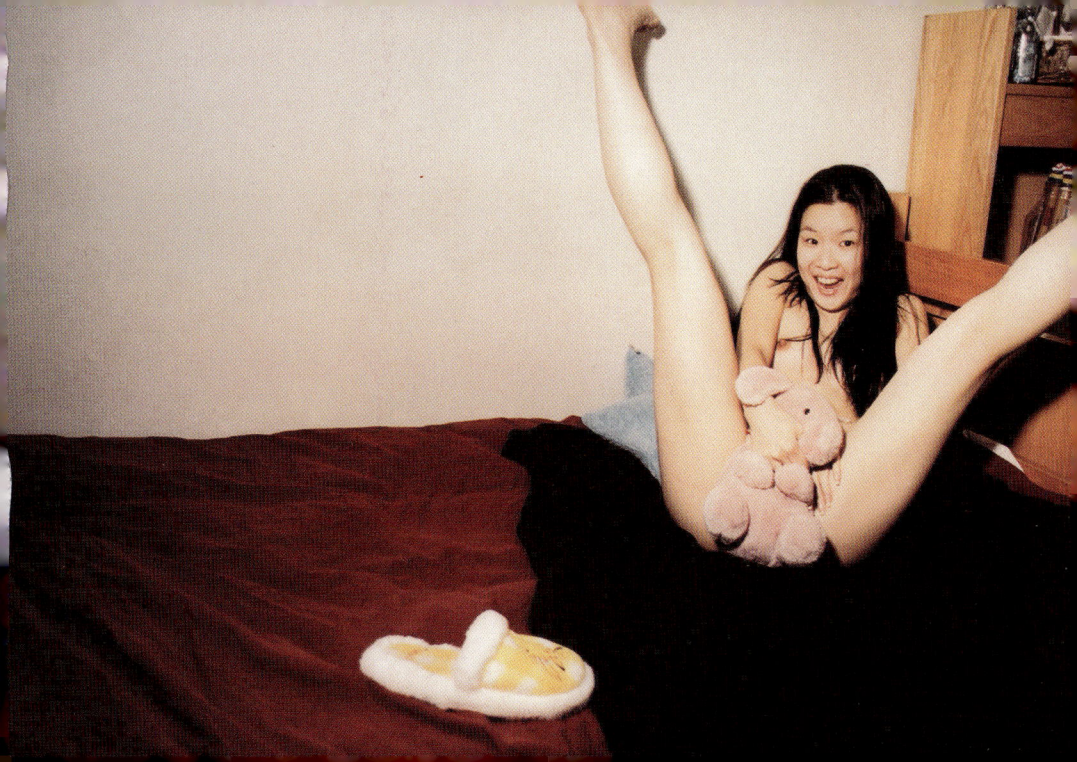

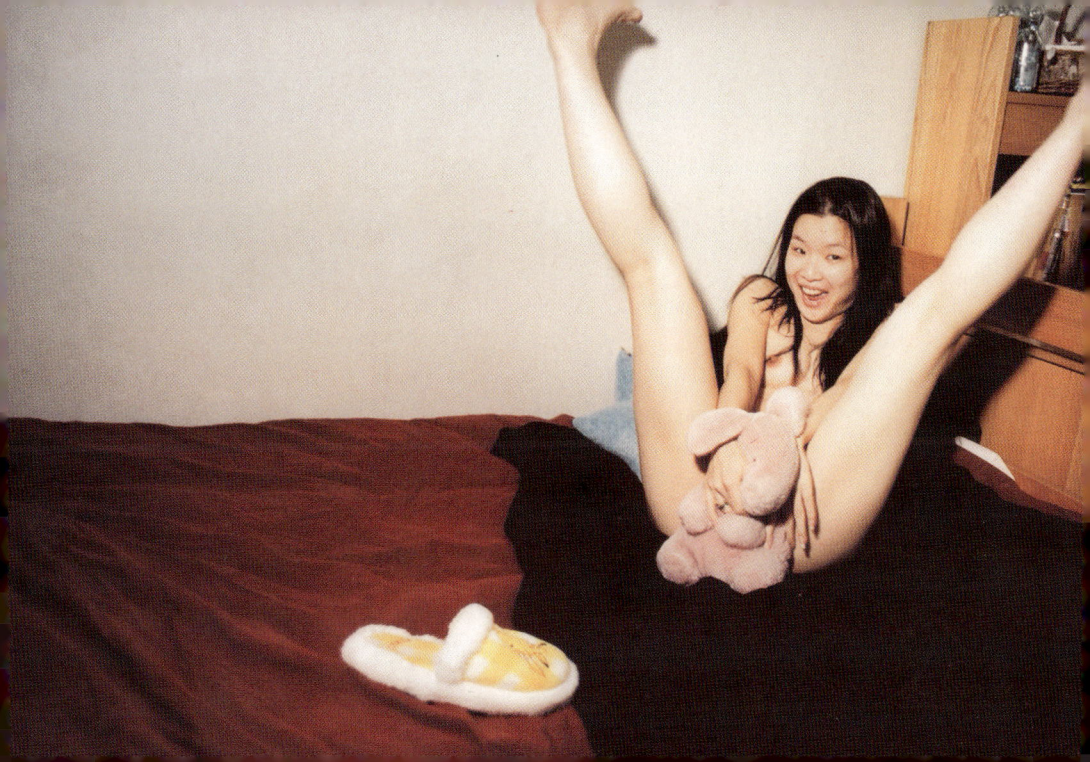

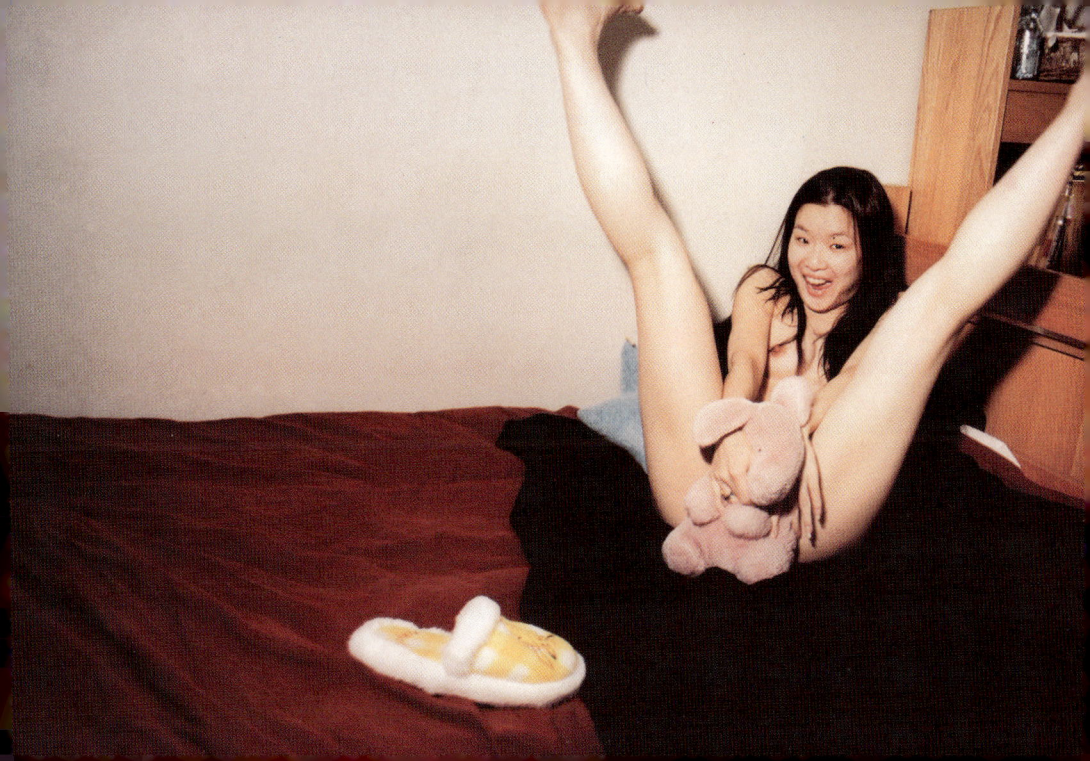

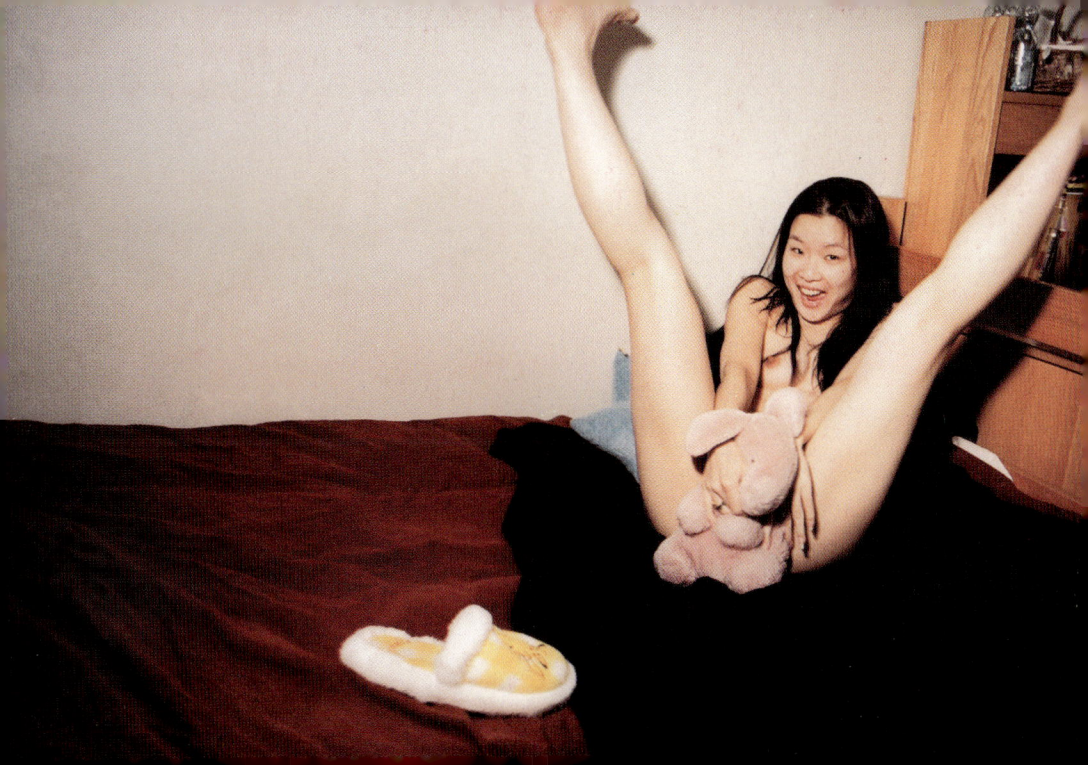

STRIP FLIPS! SUSAN

Published in the United States by powerHouse Books,
a division of powerHouse Cultural Entertainment, Inc.
180 Varick Street, Suite 1302, New York, NY 10014-4606
telephone 212 604 9074, fax 212 366 5247
e-mail: info@powerHouseBooks.com
web site: www.powerHouseBooks.com

First edition, 2001

Paperback ISBN 1-57687-127-4 (Susan)

Printed and bound by Grafiche d'Auria, Ascoli Piceno

Leslie Lyons would like to thank all STRIP FLIPS! subjects past, present, and future as
well as C-LAB and RGH NYC, without whose help this project would not have been possible.

A complete catalog of powerHouse Books and Limited Editions is
available upon request; please call, write, or take it all off before our web site.

10 9 8 7 6 5 4 3 2 1

Printed and bound in Italy